Echoing Back at You
A Decade of Social Media Poetry

Kaitlyn Bolyard

ISBN: 9798218056728

Cover illustration by: Bryce Ulmer
Library of Congress Control Number: 2018675309
Printed in the United States of America

Introduction

The poems included in this collection are collected, crafted, and inspired by statuses posted on social media. The earliest iterations may seem entirely nonsensical because my process echoed the intention of magnetic poetry, not changing the words in any way, merely rearranging them. In fact, if you're not ready for some serious nonsense, I might suggest entirely skipping the poems from 2011, but then you'd miss out on such gems as "I Am Father to the Brave Microwave" and "What I was doing 8 yrs old up in the fish sandwich." They have their own odd kind of wisdom to them, I think.

The poems from 2015 are also unique in style and subject because, instead of going to social media for my fodder, I turned to news articles instead. These use much more formal language as a result, and sometimes seem a bit stilted and less natural in their flow. At the same time, they give a great overview of some of the news and media issues at the time.

Over the years, I honed and developed my process, ending with this most recent year, 2021, which felt like a stressful sequel to 2020. From "Big Ole Mood," we get the title of this collection, with an apt depiction many of us can relate to:

"No one really walks into a walk-in cooler,
Just runs in and screams. It's a primal sort of
Self-care. A big-ole mood echoing back at you."

Kaitlyn Bolyard

There are also several poems culled from the social media of individuals. These are all dedicated to the people they were written about. Some of these people have since passed away, and I am immensely glad I have poems to remember them by.

Likewise, may we remember this past decade with lighthearted humor and give ourselves grace for our mistakes

2011
Some Hot Mess Barbie

In the Scotch Grandma
July 2

People! Someone! Hey, anyone!
I just will fire a free thanks told by a douchebag
Who will endure feather letters if by today you're
Wilsons.
I went to Eagle One sleeping.
I need coffee then, to feel I've gone.

This, like my damn burger dad and me,
Is lakefront for those never having tea,
Something really wearing a can.
Storm going from brave special knit
with my wee rolling cap that do to me
who I nip during storm.

To nothing of want today,
to else in the scotch grandma.
Possibly heard good 104 update.
Please schmooze-o-rama morning degree,
follow any world through weather.
Their excuse of exactly that hair,
stood for what Katie on Milwaukee from Facebook.

Crap my rest. End of tonight, drinking thermometer life,
got read before tonight, scared.
I stayed at disapproval statuses inside
and you like the car, so wear this time
the real-woman shorts. I always
keep at the cutest guy, to have every lakefront thing.

Kaitlyn Bolyard

A Poem on Clingy Sauna Protest
July 18

Scott, I park as God is that current.
I ride around it. He thrilled it,
My friend who can go turns, and Angie
Dodged outside, wrote on the felt:
"How out are our needs, Walker?"
Deal her protesters; I run about.

Don't include a boyfriend early,
With first the streetcar, then the week.
Got the need to exercise me.
A gift - Shalom - of heat,
But the worry center project for salons
Arrived about today. Austin was spa don't.
He's published at Better Hair Class.

I like losing one, went on to cut good
And left, feeling my thanks to the morning.
John is verse, like the accommodation
Starting in gym, everyone.
I better look forward, my day today.
York the holy stepped yesterday into my Hell.
Tonight, today, Wisconsin.

Its website week, out into yikes, cat and you.
One is hot. Two look right sick.
A poem on clingy sauna protest
when my article on Mansfield
proved too much.

Airplane to Publish Beat

I and the Google + stylist got cutting Facebook today
After watching an angry episode wherever Twilight
Unemploys hairy lions in my zone.
Simultaneously, the other class tried to crash
Me and an old lady, sending China a 2/3 economy.
Slowing the "social networking" of a farmhouse,
A little alien visited the party.
Students asked layers (but how long?) they had gotten
While home mist surges.

Early reminder: they're from Wisconsin.

I can't get it on me.
It's system is slinky and would get just me, the only of
my soul.
This made a state take-down, each time a hit until I go
down,
But is it the last?
I opened one giant door, far-spaced.
Can the ex-husband find that best fucking place?
Airplane to publish beat.
Think to their conversation. Bitch it about.
Snow feeds the heat between my might.
It's on creepy. I'd take being over this Twitter doctor,
son.
Who's going venturing?

Kaitlyn Bolyard

Me, Shit, and the First Smoking Recruiter

Had a meeting in 2011
To backdrop the Florida sky
To free every recent "do not quit,"
Holy with the diving comedies.
Their good deal or scary air force is like
Me, shit, and the first smoking recruiter.
Salary today: these single-morning U.S. Presidents,
No salary cigarettes. Even my state is good.
I will require the flowers retired.

Try the 26th movie, got one house
Doing more smut, the drug testing.
Boo. I lost this August and Q101.
That lavender is looking ready for a fuck,
Like when applying to see thirty blues
For an episode. Little tired.

Hello, pure great 19. Are you applying that heat?
Want romance for that Juliette-time party?

I am Father to the Brave Microwave
July 20

When all thought is good, how a need grows!
This is going great. New grief did the guy my way.
To you authors just considering photos,
I am father to the brave microwave.
She knows who I look to, Taco Bell new theory.

Miss Possible Amazon is the cutest disapproval running,
judging.
Prepare, going like you look against the bed.
This thing starts tomorrow and I already
Have a friend's rented happy,
Should never wear Don Draper's stop.

Can't busy baby Wirch sleep?

This is good, is for the hour.
I am all-day adorable, five o'clock morning.
Buy shorts, sneezing a weak Milwaukee hooka,
hoping that and that.

Will our leftovers just shadow someone?

Kaitlyn Bolyard

McDoucherson wanted a day to poop

Double haha!
Dear 30 excited douchy quizzes,
Yes, what I seriously love is that McDoucherson wanted
a day to poop.

There is no May morning to get beautiful good. When
rainbows matter, are sunsets why I open so good? So go
take my yes, find this song. It absolutely out-scams 2
keyless puppy challenges. At System Baha'i, all staff
don't mother. We are becoming a loving morning where
nature grows. Was the entry in this storm closed?

Try for members. I only friend the very best two with
way more going on the way to famous system kittens and
something far. I even woke remote Whitewater to wake
for a tight different start up pop.

Post it if we got up tomorrow coupling this. You're ever
born a day late. Style then to tell them since yesterday
here's loose. Would you do coupling, honey? The Will I
love decided pictures in gag.

Ground up, just beef to textbooks on the seat

I'm Polpettone, 16. I'm long so Ripieno is my son.
I recover hard and come in loveseats,
tired recently of my son boiled, yeah if good eggs.
I decided the weeks people started that conclusion:
forgot recovering and 4 George to celebrate the addition.
I want that again.

We surrounded every two tired days with something I
ate.
I'm free from Martin's day, relaxing to it.
She loves me leading a game and going first of thrones,
ground up, just beef to text books on the seat. Think it.
Celebrate people, the Italians have gone.
I'm so sausage, I dish a nice comfort to decide this.
It doesn't really chase the day and food,
nice to be recently mesh curb, clearly that beautiful guy
leading.

For if up well before morning, to the corner to be with
you,
to give the world, that's with WANT of you, okay?
Reading, celebrate Sunday, our want "normal."

Seven huge Italian people, something every holiday,
and pine and birthday, and later have spinach, a mouse.
Why nothing this week - a day booked west with why -
bend me to cookie without prosciutto, then
an offer of provolone, settled leading.

Know how any good suggestion tastes
July 26

1. Be vague.
2. Read Frank's apparently excited status.
3. To update on this, see line 3.
4. Play August at Super Do-Better.
5. Discover that angry market-about eyesore with any Wisconsinite in the ridiculous wonder of yore.
6. Find out why the next us is nature, an awkward camper.
7. Eat natural things of food, eat Kenosha, eat things.
8. Network up like the time star.
9. Saturday, with that back-way morning, know how any good suggestion tastes.
10. Solve a casting comment we are all about at the hotel YMCA.
11. Mark in black here another square year atmosphere.
12. On that problem, you and everybody in Chicago on Sunday come in again.
13. Shout with the people.
14. On our afternoon morning, tell friends now coming to get back when you give 3-4 lists.
15. Stuff Emma with - here's it for what it, my better, what.
16. With more done, be us, just as it is for we bought these tasks.
17. Ask for gas, for a good boyfriend.

The debt ceiling crashing into the stadium
July 27

Good morning, Dad.

Let's go to the YMCA and talk about John Boehner, who looks like a leathery Muppet. Now that there is going to be a season a few weeks from now, everyone can get stuff done with pig skins and pads and their shins. As long as the debt ceiling doesn't come crashing into the stadium. I somehow finished the mountain of dishes. About to make some fantasy football bids.

Soon I will be the only person in my department debating YOUR and YOU'RE - learn the difference! Sometimes I want to be like a cat person, really immature, beating up sluts. For those that have been asking: this is one of those moments when I feel like I need to get away from Wisconsin. Even I forget to punctuate and abbreviate properly. This is where I ask: Do all cats have a sixth toe on their front paws?

I got to go to bitchin rock shelters in Canada a couple days ago. It's complete now; here it is. What a good morning!

Go on now. I am closing my wall to just about everyone. Even my boyfriend on Facebook. Nothing personal.

P. S. Guess who officially got taken out for a spin

Kaitlyn Bolyard

I can't believe my hand
July 28

I can't believe my hand, share it instead of telling,
about to embark like a boss who's got an idea
in hand. It's an awesome meatloaf recipe switching
time, went on a covert clean up, isle so hopefully.
When Jaguar driving Thursday and Friday,
my mission is someone who rides lanes tomorrow.

He wakes up tiptoeing into my hate, when a motorcycle
how they make turns, or stay on your car's can fast!
A special day to share? Don't side with him,
he'll be surprised! My pants yo, just raise
your stop faster than you care about.
Last day at my son's room with pulling out.
Keep your eyes on someone who rides.

For him tomorrow I shart :/ dangerous as it is
on the road on the...road. Ahh, thunder,
especially turning corners and OFF your don't.
Follow too a motorcycle, please, the clinic.
The balloons and streamers look twice before
a drive repost. SHARE closely, bikes can be heading
to Racine CELL phones! If the ROAD you disabled for
...can't tell you I am not -- I am SUPERabled.

What I was doing 8 yrs old up in the fish sandwich

I need to Care For Kids. I believe they
Train Your 8 yr old...I WANT STEAK!"
Hoping the storms take the kids. I've been
Safety House @ the world! trying to learn
good morning fb. I didn't really work always.
Grace Lutheran Church is showing "How
Dragon." :)

this piece for making me have
and want to be a Virgin" was just thinking about
what I was doing 8 yrs old up in the fish sandwich
it meant so much though... my cubicle! Moving
made better by learning to cook for so many
years... Thank you Madonna though I suppose
we haven't yet!!! ;)

when "Like a Name Plaque" played.
Has NIN ever taught a man for a day
that wasn't sexy? Teach a man that
my future hubby :)

So I've decided to FREE
Movies and Glee for a conversation without...
Don't remember just got a world!
made a song by fishing, he eats to fish,
he eats Indian dishes will hold off where dear friend
will sell you that fish I really wish :)

Kaitlyn Bolyard

Add eggs to Benadryl
July 29

I'm getting psyched my face hurts :) Awww
play I'd just waked up to discover how to see?
It's a pretty biopsy this morning. I am surprised
a good day an hour after the hospital
Gaah day celebrating my allergy list!
swollen shut and all is cruel punishment
bud Johnny holding these guys. I pee a little
one and hives all last week, I work

Hooray! Khalakka has a wine glass yeah baby
and eat/drink until we are working It's ok
add eggs to Benadryl eyes are over his trunk
Black Coffee) officially been given crack/call
little choked up "Yep. And what with such a

Happy Black Art Day! You have a poem, wise
Had a wonderful help by cleaning Dante didn't
on that! to paint Fedor's bad mood. Time better
night of my having a gig also pays
short discussion about big bucks (like
freestyle out they name national holiday
the gig will think the Universe of those

be in a Woot! I need a Technical College in
Mom is out Woo! Hopefully I am "Packing/Moving
don't wake up as one of the subs involved
(everything is). The qualifications required
class at Gateway is not communication
been frustrating you? & it almost made me

up to play can plus the first episode of
mood before enjoying the day also makes it
girl wash her own mighty morphin power

16

son's birthday. Got your son." I'm still
when I asked a phenomenal kid. :) drop
20). times over the just had one at work

keys for Larry and I almost found another
to do some work. Driivving takes forever!!
tonight at 8 imitable Scotty on my
I love Larry's drums. If they go hang with
for the first Racine. it is playing a ice-breaker
than a better Inferno. Friday September 9th
Key West. : (bad day at figuring out
what is or wants me in something that's

boyfriend's couch by shattering a ranger!
is because I'm all he had this time.
stuff and he's nothing new there (AKA
my best butt! Boo: She should be a nail
Oral Interpersonal Communications at 6:00 pm
down bottom end woke me up permission to
as only he wouldn't let me laugh so much

someone is full! running around. See more
if I can and he said, so very blessed to do
Hemingway has shown every one of
up randomly several of those moments where
as he was trying to find the simple answer

Kaitlyn Bolyard

I am broker wearing normal clothes

August 16

WI state districts get errands done.
Phones HATE the process.
It's true what Rascal had.
Have decided, guys, to do the musical number.
Realizing my day started in "Gamer," down again.
Will never understand why the interview went well.
12 and 22 growing her hair.
They say the lake rebels out on the new song, "Pine Sol."
Should know better.
I wish I saw a girl.
I am broker wearing normal clothes.
Make sure to check out 39%.
How I love beautiful weather out!
Pregnancy emotions and/or instead of women being concerned.
Not only did the wrong foot channel, it is fantastic to wear the vote in Kenosha.
Get out and grill out with cravings...
Urr...calling to complain with their age.
He walked along when I spilled grammar.
White to orientation today, then broke and a fake teacher.
Vote TODAY, my honey...
Well at least no matter what service did this, the beach cranberry juice is everywhere.
Subscribe, and feel thee anyone.
But if I asked Liam somewhere...

The same small club that just swaps plums

A little like being a turd in a punchbowl,
blissfully participating in
the American civic religion of statism.
A downer, a crank, a loonie, a jerk,
a positive evil about uncomfortable facts,
the indistinguishable nature of large vested interests.

Their state-enabled exploitation,
the same small club that just swaps plums.
Electronic voting gizmos bully and plunder us
with abandon, and you'd rather we had
a dictatorship experienced as an
emotional act, willful denial.
To murderously lord it over the entire planet,
one particular region of tyranny,
like a badge of moral superiority.

Border on zero, also bright blue
adding to the pile, despite his high negatives.
Math makes a pretty cut.
Expressive voting decreases my impact.
The corrupt crowd will suddenly stop stealing.

Splashing a seductive performance,
prompting deep thoughts,
dragged herself out under duress,
her one and only, she said mournfully.

One of the lower matchups, this earth judging,
like he did in that clip.
As much of a cunt as he currently is,

19

Kaitlyn Bolyard

gassing up like a legend.
Go outside of this small circle once in a while

Naked people have little or no influence
August 17

Finishing my cup of coffee
(indicates the table where the volunteers sit
with the large books of names).
Anyone else notice that regressives are all doom and
gloom?
HAPPY 30TH BIRTHDAY TO MY BIG BRO
then heading out to the farmer's market.
Me: "but it's not required" BEST ROOMIE EVER
They prey on people's fears like late-night commercials
for weight loss and boner pills.

Does anyone agree with me that the bookstore stinks?
I'm in a very good mood for them,
him: "uh...no." That's why I'm gonna be
buying my books from Amazon this year.

Ok, create your own homemade pizza,
pots & pans, starting August 22 pizza crusts
& a tea kettle will be on sale at SuperValue.
And I kind of feel like sharing me:
"So you DON'T need it." The sky is always falling.

Don't have to shove my $$$ down a toilet
now that I am partially moved in and more stuff
gathered,
makes it a million times.
Clothes make the man. Him: "...no?"
And they only seem to celebrate when they "win"
elections
or take away the rights of some group
or another on 80th Street.
Naked people have little or no influence in society.

Kaitlyn Bolyard

Me: "no." Don't have to stand in line for
you know 'bout an hour...
Here is my updated need list in Kenosha.
Just had a conversation with a poll worker:
"For Jesus" says Oatmeal Lake 2011.
Living room chair is here!
If you're parting with any of these items,
anyone heard about the new gold's gym that's coming?
Decided to be a "rebel" elderly gentleman volunteer:
"...and we'll need to see an ID."

Why is depressing paranoia so popular?
Bookcase/shelves let me know I'm thinking of joining.
Some people couldn't do my job and instead
of calling to complain about service,
my son had a dentist's appointment yesterday.
Me: "you'll NEED to see it?" Lamps.

Yesterday I lost my gym membership to razor
and now I'm looking at options,
working with the families I work with,
did the opposite and is always *really* nervous.
Him: "well, it'll make things go a lot faster up there."
A microwave saw the Three Mile Island
cooling towers this morning
who care so much for their kids.

Turtle love has a piece of pig in it
August 18

Try to flush the stones for breakfast.
Housekeeping comes at 2.
No daycare today, so my girlies are going to
shower, eat, and then head to the pub.
Is this what being a mother feels like?

Oatmeal is like underwear.

Here are the rules:
1. Know the taste/texture of meat.
2. Plunge in the first five minutes.
3. I can do it better.
Now to drive myself to work.

Turtle love has a piece of pig in it.

Trading multi-tasking to step down for
long lady days.
Ready for tonight?
I am humbled, now stop being so fussery!
Back to Canadian bed and we'll glow,
get pepper sprayed, and play pong.

Life's not in text words, off the bars, discovered.
On account of apathy, I'm taking the girls
to a wedding on Wednesday.
My sister is being admitted this weekend.

Why do banana walnut muffins rise before my alarm?

Kaitlyn Bolyard

Everything on feelings, love, and donations is happy. Just have a conversation.

Feels good to be easily irritated
August 22

Our government is - today - the cutest job to watch.
So, if anything new runs after the ice cream truck,
open mic starts taking my brain out of my head.
Minecraft prepared me for the history of this place.
Everyone who made it came over,
Rick-rolled twice and looked at strollers.
The Tetris block has fallen to break free.
Feels good to be easily irritated by happy birthday greetings,
and Friday night baking sucks.

Slaughtered by grilled cheese and weeds
November 14

Come in to assemble a bookshelf too big for me to read.
I just lost. Oh coffee – don't splash me.
Watch tonight's Packers/Vikings game. Or fail me now
and hate football.
The game totally found an "everything that annoys you"
mode.
Was feeling all artist statement for working again
tonight.
Dishes and dinner, pants that fit, just sitting down to
eat.
Top-chef like, grinding, watching the game, did laundry,
Getting into the can't, doing it because they're human.
Find the gay time four months ago and we're all a touch
of the same.
I'm going to really enjoy playing with person artforms,
with war.
Sea salt, ya dig?
I will give sometimes the world as a Christmas present
Or less than maybe someone's several dollars.
5 hours, the time anyone wants to feel way too big.
Come over and the recall will begin to help me.

A friend's bush full of futsal

December 6

Dear Zynga, fix yesterday. It is easier, whenever I start.
I now own a tough day, a construction project.
The huz is out of the awesome ZUMBA gold.
Why should I? Apparently, in reading up on my son, I must ask
Please! Is this for 10 days? I have been here now.
"I'm not going as Yusuf...just as Cat Stevens."
Couldn't find a completed manuscript.

Farmville, STOP judging out-of-town work from home.
I think to save just 3 facts.
Office people are very Sims Social...I tiptoe through life.
The widely stateside is real good, as ever.
Listening to him only to arrive was my favorite,
A piece of myself, "what would punchable faces have to trim?"
And Mom is in the car, safely at death HAVING QUESTS!!
The 12-0 Packers, unknown int'l sport,
A friend's bush full of futsal till due date.

Waiting for a long job today, so live by donating.
Fruit snacks are always a first.
To understand Imhotep, do time, enjoy being home
Doing blood like crack. SQUEEE! Tribal belly dance -
Time for everything. Are we going? When we're in, back to basics,
In heaven, some hot mess Barbie on her way lately,
playing Lexulous.

Kaitlyn Bolyard

2012

The Gods Wait to Delight in Her

Kaitlyn Bolyard

We both share at least one god
January 11

Got bad news: two cats or one Katie bashed his plans.
Not much is going right. What say you?
I'm liking this one thing: his 2010 campaign.

With you in mind, CNN's Dana leveraged his increasing
support.
After his second-place finish, he has what it takes to
love.
The best so far was bringing Illinois and Wisconsin
together now.

It's so nice that you're proud of me.
For me, people of Bookface, I am doing everything for
me.
Love and miss you. Got an exclusive interview moving
forward.

Sis, go to South Carolina and plan to spend all day
outside.
In New Hampshire, be the Republican nominee.
One at a time love you, Madeline.

Reek of sophistication. I mean there is nothing wrong
with that.
For the life of me, that shit's sexy.
Our route, 4.2 miles. Woot!

Rest in peace with Rep. Ron Paul. Tell us if you think in
the snow.
Last night, the mixed reports about Gov. Walker

eventually died.
His team is being caught on this issue.

We share the same commonality: sharing updates.
We both have at least one god.
Did the official Google map of us.

Criminal governors finally took the time to educate the
public.
I don't know why they would have such a strong
aversion.
Venereal diseases have to get musical education.

Cheri, Megan, Erika, et. al. turn out ass cheek tattoos.
Add femininity, a lower back/ass tattoo, call it a "tramp
stamp."
I wonder if Corretta had one.

Truth doesn't remember
January 12

I feel like typical Kenosha, everything waiting.
They all stopped.
There must be a sign overhead: Clouds Beware.

I agree with most messages,
But I may not agree with you without a trip to the walk-in
Where you can pin me to a 2008 calendar.

Lick your own crotch and drool.
Don't remember bad times or bite things in May.
Keep my germs and we can have a wonderful
relationship.

You're all tired, my 20-year Boy Scout.

You believe about your beliefs.
It's not just the way you're delivered to church.
You're one of the few people with God.

Yes. Yes. Yes.
Hanging out a day or two late.
Everything you say will work.
The way you lived your life wasn't broken.
Truth doesn't remember who you used to be.

By the time I get home, my paper for myself will have
died

And the clocks on the wall will stop seeming smarter.

First black man on my shuffle

Officially employed again.
I love love love very interesting and little-known Black
History.
Happy birthday Jessica!
When the track sung by the Bangles
made it out best, this chicken could cause a wreck.
Fact...Jasper Honeycutt pops up on this recipe.
OUCH!! I'm one year away from gorgeous.
Homer: "Mmmm...Donuts!"

In bed, taking bondage photos.
A paradigm shift - first black man on my shuffle.
I just wanted to limit my statuses.
Too old today for a walk.
Two teachers were by the lake today, editing photos.
Here's the entire outdoor lewd act with my little lady.

To put it on children, I just got a 2FL article
until I am arrested this week for a friend.
Step 2. Eliminate requests from the cast of Twilight.
Now, let's go. It was about 3 episodes, it seems,
since I cried about what I'm celebrating.
Halftime with Madonna on something. Say thank you
with accusations of thinking about you.

Step 1. Highlight this week's American Life.
Track down that moment.
I was due to reflect on NCIS.
Doing the 200th episode, taking a look.

(blank of course)
February 9

In 1972, a green town I love choked
on the mist of an economic equilibrium.
It deteriorated under awesome chocolate
shared with the Joker.
We destroyed the Gotham hierarchy.

A person digging for the prison
by a good, all-time favorite (aw yeah!)
went to military court for a good night in Washington.

Many people remember the doctor
told them to take doggie greeting cards
and send them to the debate.
I finally got well after this diagnosis:
crack commando unit.
Thursday afternoon is a lovely time for life.

At a gay marriage, frozen watermelon
created complete chaos (blank of course).

Hoping for a god who sits still is like
singing to a fallen soldier with swollen cheeks.
The Decemberists ordered sinus infections.
If I walk to the tavern in Waukegan,
an open mic still surrounds that sound.

An MRI running a memory
April 5

Glucose syrup makes parents come to burn.
Here is this, I have a candle.
The dresser with my baby will be in next week's
breaking news.

But it's me, Katrina.
Have mercy on my hair.
The beautician tells me her highest moment.
This is a far cry from chillaxin, alright guys?

Looking sick for a jumpy tomorrow.
Check out these nice sheets.

On this year's event page, wear the fancy jealousy.
Exclusive first-look photos of Vincent flirting.
Brittany is giving lingerie to every woman.

Mow the lawn message for Obama.
Trouvaille du jour: a free portrait.

An MRI running a memory
Of your pet prison for shooting him
And one of cognitive at Montreal.

Kaitlyn Bolyard

First Night of Whiskey and Love
October 2

I was Mary and (with other additions)
the best on the Pumpkin Patch.
I was told Tim seriously likes that race between
wedding and roof.
October is a first hayride, atmospheric Fanfare,
inactive debate.

Tonight, windows take my Detroit and poise,
rouse from ancient slumber.
I find a companion, one of the best.
I do it on a Cthulhu horror movie.

This is where Little Z and I see it,
love deleted for practicing with guys.
Seven "friends" could prepare a great night
to surpass what I am to do.
Sure, I don't know if Ohio, with everyone in my style,
"likes" her.

It's 2012, Tina Fey is most likely to tell you
Romney's jokes and I hate being awesome.

Cutting Quantum Tattoos

October 4

Having police for last night's clusterfluff
was not connected with pickles.
A black kitty watched the pussy eat.
Off the first debate, this guy worth dying for
leaped around the place.

Today, I love tonight, reading holy fire,
Thinking of the man whole,
Ways to go to rehab.
Milwaukee casts Hulu on Mt. Pleasant and
You know the constitution of love.

The department of small steps picked
Franklin to do the script.
I'm cutting quantum tattoos,
Running with Rudolph and Romney,
Pissed off and interested.

Kaitlyn Bolyard

An Unofficial Message
October 7

They say that weird people ruin God,
Like underneath they play twisted ways.
I know a few of us look at all that bullshit,
And realize if everyone would question the past,
It would stir up such a hunger.

A bunch of yesterdays cannot leave you satisfied.
No heat can open the future.
On our turf, the celebration is difficult to bottle.
It is that wine on my brain knitting words
In my heart tonight.

Things made into responsibilities let work get better.
Throw something in your life,
Like water, coffee, or history.
Finally wear out carpet flags in the Chicago apartment,
Taste every terrible interaction,
And don't ask about official messages on Sundays.

A Nice Change
October 8

OK, I'm a nice change from great "American" holidays,
A pretty classical celebration, not funny at all.
A person, a man, a little boy poking out of the cold
weather,
thinks about biscuits and gravy on my head.
But it's not funny.

I'm positive God kicks the crap out of Columbus
For haunting slaughterhouses.
I hear natives raped, tortured, and killed on the radio.
Happy Doom Day, everyone!

Isn't it great to fall behind and face the morons
Who didn't find enough love?
If they had such a ginormous wedding venue, I want to
think
this civil union of two friends put our differences aside.
To finance the pile and new additions, dictators stayed
with
wonderful, nice young men, meeting again in the
hardware store.

And the dungeon was amazing. A great ten days followed
by
Early dinner, one piece of a gas leak.
Now it's time to shower.
The mania they threw him in rocked past logic.

Sometimes we have to accomplish an expedition,
a bigger goal, deal out a few hours to ready a busy day.
Please look, keep leafing through what you follow,
and get this studied.

Kaitlyn Bolyard

From her thong to the risk of birthday wind

I swear: fuck you.
We are popping today, homesick for atheists.
God cursed Facebook for cooking Missouri's Jesus.
Music suggests I might tell a friend "It is what you say
that matters."
In an interview, local news reporters described love,
highlighting reckless attacks in our hometowns.
Playing the young lady, I believe these adjectives sound
like
Nuclear devastation. Convince me otherwise.

The Day After the Election
November 7

A fabulous man had super powers,
Meat candy, and wine.
I always knew Obama trusted
Drinking, fucking, and breathing.

Mr. President, a few people
Watch the results, trust news organizations,
Love Facebook.
You are just another word for bacon.

So happy the best projections say
A woman and a lesbian, Tammy Baldwin,
Is probably coming or going down right now
With such integrity.

What I'm seeing is like a fart
Accidentally using feedback,
Sighing relief today.

Election's over.
The people polling in Wisconsin
Post anything political on Facebook,
Vote for the rarest large mammal in the world.

The pimp is president, calling me: hey, hey!
I usually don't get sleepy, but right now
I must not be doing projections.
Obama, walk out, give your speech,
Drop the mic!

Kaitlyn Bolyard

Learning How to Eat like Julia Child
November 30

Holy Christmas tree,
I love my hand, who I met on pilgrimage
Visiting these places,
And I actually fit in because being a lezzy is
Called the fun theory.

Edible friends are awesome
If they sleep in, gargle garlic, and try everything.
The prostate is clean and happy.
Amazing people affected by poetry say last night
Will just go down, full of win.

Rudolph, needless drivel, and balls
Are mission impossible,
Closing to all my pissed-off requests.
I'm sick of seeing
Toothaches, you, that gallery, coffee cups,
Watching hydrogen peroxide genocide.

My mixed threads, bogged down by Scotland,
Don't put up with fiercely hammering your
Bacon on my cheek. Some might say
Home is learning where to eat.

Her Fearless Heart
December 4

When did you have black photos?
Before the wedding?

Terminal cancer has one week to propose.
Love happens now, in an attempt to be polite.

Several prints are sexy, the love of his life,
A sweet fiancée.
People stop, love this, vow to marry,
Comment on this image.

She isn't done yet.
Important artwork
Before three horrible letters,
A future quest finally complete.

Top-Secret Christmas Mission
December 7

My day is off feeling morning,
Straightening weather data,
And warming a woman dismantled.
My stories about first-stop pre-ordered January
Tempt her excitement.

I might not be forgotten.

Today, the world fought bravely,
Epic time flossed conversations,
The theatre creased my thoughts.
The intensity of family feuds flashed
During the first week
Of me and my sisters going to Gurnee,
Missing mom riding along.

The top-secret Christmas mission,
An event bravely bitten,
Quit within twenty minutes.
Equal poems compare global fiction,
Short, planned nights.
Anybody stabbed with scissors
Knows this season.

Stashing the Joy

December 20

In 1951, love dreams of having this year,
Entertaining witness protection,
Drinking with a friend.
But does anybody really have a good night?
Where does Rosemary stash the joy?

We aren't even going to be happy with Christmas.
If this "snow" keeps up, those who pray
Will make us pull over and cry.
The suffering is over.

This half-naked lady, a really cute montage,
Walked right into the lamp post.
Her ripped dress, silenced until tomorrow,
Looks like the Brothers Grimm.
Outside the house, she sleeps well,
Touched up by a snowy afternoon.

Kaitlyn Bolyard

Epic Design Time
December 27

for Bryce

For the past couple of years, he has loved
Official salad, different soup, super printers,
And Hanukkah contests, especially ones with
Epic design time.
He ate caloric intake and bought save-the-dates,
Spent morning quotes on wedding stationary.

Yesterday, things he made
Moved onto paper and envelopes:
Cool pictures for the printing.
New turbines got their first look
At portfolios, coloring gin and tonics.

Now he is going to be a veggie, getting quotes,
Shaping wrapped Twinkies with a
Wedding day monogram.

The Next Martha Stewart

for Ashley

She fries five million shallots
And buys a wedding ring.
She squeals on a train
While wearing the wrong shoes.
She loves spending time with
An afternoon Christmas,
Expensive presents, beautiful music.
She feels public market tacos,
Avoids the bomb,
And honors the victims.

When China knows the national mood,
Only one man is capable of sharing
Wine with her at the art museum.
The rarest large mammal in the world
Provides nice scenery for their voting.

She gets Old Milwaukee breakfast for free
With good karma.
Her winning Whole Foods spirulina
Welcomes back a fatty soulmate
With Krispy Kremes.
This health freak couldn't find groceries.

Oh god, looking at the remnants of cookies,
She decides to give second chances.

Kaitlyn Bolyard

Where You Find Love
December 28

for Sara

Only she holds an idea twice,
Everything spinning,
Astounded by direction.
A true mother, feeling orange,
Ready to choose between
Happy, free, confused and lonely.

Truly honest, sometimes
It can't be said

Because kisses and farts don't care
Where you find love.
And all those other people have no idea,
Blame it on getting lost.

This girl has sunburn in her eyes.
She will break you.
In her head, the best men
Move both today and tomorrow.
In her heart, she says
A perfectionist smiles with her hands.
Her six-year-old daughter's handwriting
Announces crazy laughter.

All Milton, All the Time

for Milton

This remark is a few days late.
He resembles Ghostbusters
And people I know.
He watches snow,
Doesn't recall traveling,
Discovering this bed.
He is such a bastard
But actually brilliant.

He can go away to audition,
Grab a script,
And respond to recent events.
He misses important messages and
Winter weather advisories.

He's done nothing but dream.

Kaitlyn Bolyard

We Can Talk About Her Now
December 29

for Emily

Simply genius,
Her unnecessarily large words
Make people jump.
A tortoise sleeps in her windowsill.

Sitting on the couch by herself,
She miscalculates sickness and misses
The end of the world.

She looks for the Mayans,
Draws a white elephant
For a 2013 calendar.

This collective amnesia
Rattles her picture window.

Distraction in December
December 30

for Karla

Wide awake, outside
Smoking a cigarette,
Swearing to Jesus,
Wearing night
In her neighbor's backyard.
This isn't as funny when
Buildings glow in the dark.

A new dress on New Year's,
The strangest fucking safely tucked
In the basement too many nights
In a row.

She realizes good people want church,
Have heard American dinosaurs laughing.

She walks, hungry,
The gods waiting to delight in her.
The wind hints that ideas
Are cold this time of year.

Kaitlyn Bolyard

2013

No Complex Assembly Required

Kaitlyn Bolyard

Made for Current Usage

January 3

for Megan

She lives where she can barely afford
Ugly spice for the new year.
That means she has to claim dresses
From fellow nerds.
Her kids came in the mail.

Addictive bath salts will increase
Super Mario's spice,
But she doesn't want psyched
Disrespect in the house.

Homemade water costs
A bead-weaving set and
Sporty baby stuff.
Chicken n' rice soup is supposed to
Move the galaxy.
Dinner increases bullshit,
Is quietly sobbing to itself.

The bill is so much that
She is a little extended into
Sacrifice.
Hell is playing round two
Nine times.

Perfect on the Outside
January 14

for Alexandria

She is pounding, planning, placing,
On the wide scale, waiting, listening,
Everything for the wedding.
At 10 am, a possible bridesmaid dress fits
The faces of the kids from Korea.
That fancy fail cools overnight.

Barely Monday this morning,
Happy coffee makes her OCD friend grateful.
No complex assembly required.
This girl gleefully described three inches.
She needs strong people to load heavy things.

Kaitlyn Bolyard

2014

I Have to Tell You

So Quickly
May 1

I started two jobs,
So much to do,
Of course the real ovaries
Got paid.
I can use grammar correctly,
It's my fun, but money
Is always a job.
Very grateful I can get paid
To be me.

Iowa was leaving,
Drenched in Lionel Shrivner.
If we had both,
It would be time to send
Snarky emails right now.

Yeah, the Barnes and lonely.
No seriously, I don't feel like
Getting fourteen visitors
With big eyes, trying to hang out.
No wonder I'm having
A hard time.
Trying to do this.

Filled out poems for the sounds
I still want, trying to be
Surrounded by so many rhymes
So quickly.

I Believe in Open Lines
October 5

Dracula was the first blood relative I ever knew.
We watched a Tim Burton double feature
At the cookie factory.
Our roadside rescue bunny ate an amputee at the haunt.
You have a mythical creature hidden inside you,
So never be ashamed of your love for fire.
They impose their feelings on the rest of us,
So sometimes you just have to dance it out
And unpack the wall lockers.
I'm somewhat gay, but my girlfriend's really gay.
I'm glad to report they removed my dad's chest tubes.
I know you're a feminist, and I think that's adorable.
I am honored you woke up every thirty minutes last
night
Just to talk to me, and I have to tell you
Pluto got declared a planet again.

Kaitlyn Bolyard

2015
Illegally Remembering

Kaitlyn Bolyard

Sitting on Radar Alarm Posts
January 15

Talking about jihad, holy war
Linguistic struggling and striving
Agents arrested him before he put
His alleged plot into action, articles telling him
How skeletons plot out a children's picture book
Or seven-part epic series

He ostensibly tweeted, hatched a scheme
Similar to Hebdo at a key
Posts sympathizing with terrorists led
To blowing up the Capitol with pipe bombs

In panicked flight, they gunned down high school
students
A specialized service catering to specific needs
Areas pre-determined with business questions

He prepared his partner, researched bomb-making
Purchased 600 rounds of ammunition
Smuggled turtles, grenades, meat cleavers and
Human skull fragments

A person must be sufficiently affected
There must be a case or controversy, injury in fact
Concrete relationships can be traced to independent
relief

A Pickup Truck, Abandoned
January 16

Stretched into a new state
Tremendously diverse dichotomy
Communities set in a rural suburban climate
Conservative values blend with liberal ideals

A unique political platform
World famous for size and power
The most significant city in the world
Upstate and downstate, lifestyle with aspirations

Teens on the run since January
Days have passed since your birthday, calculate
The amount of time until your baby's due date
The eastern part of what is now the United States

Surveillance showed them traveling
In a stolen red 2006 Toyota Tacoma
A firearm inside, cartridge gunpowder

Recovered in Georgia
Within walking distance of abandonment

Kaitlyn Bolyard

Runaway Kentucky
January 19

On a Florida beach, he watched young swimmers.
Urged them to reveal, instructed them to spend
Another tax hike from the highlight reel.

President Obama loomed into his final two
Midterms. Republican victories gave hopefuls
A surge of bids and impractical jokers.

With an iron rod through his head,
A man calmly surveyed four thieves breaking
A married couple's residence.

Trails of light, sightings, flying saucers
Poured over declassified documents
After decades of alleged UFO and extraterrestrial
Sightings, free and alternative.

Choose a template suitable for advanced users.
A New York rabbi died Sunday morning,
Blamed on freezing rain, a Muslim in Dresden.

Local police confirmed two battalions of
Russian soldiers crossed the border.
Pro-Moscow rebels battled an anti-terrorist operation.

Yemen's minister attempted clashes
Near the presidential palace, fired on the motorcade,
Driving him into hiding.

An airport director's private jet claimed Payne.

Chinese Vendors
January 27

Recovery from rigorous exercise
Depletes fluid that cushions and lubricates.
Connective tissue is clinically proven
To replenish rapid stiffness.

I am trying to run, but I expire in 7 days.
I have professional permission to lock my account.
My library is empty. This happened magically.

How can I change? How did this happen?
Many questions, happy weeks and ideas make me
wonder.
I want to produce on a massive scale
Sell "maybe" like a craft beer. It doesn't hurt to be
More tasty and popular.

Rolling back thousands of recipes with
Millions of lovable customers, I now demand
Indian cuisine revolving around North America.
Chinese vendors on the streets garner quick recipes.

Kaitlyn Bolyard

Commonly Consumed
January 28

We re-released propaganda
Urging murder, serious rampages in Paris.
Police killed three Islamists before they
Paralyzed hostages, killed innocents.

In recent years, we explained ideas well.
We included examples, concrete, practical
Comprehensible theories. Look at people
Who need to believe. No one can physically touch
God. Science cannot prove existence.

Doubt is even less likely to visit Moscow.
Russia's decision, one of the myriad reasons,
Published a decree. We now ban descriptions.
A retaliatory tool publicly opposes dubious activities.

I'd like to say a few words. We made a commitment to
Reduce food commonly consumed by children.
Including fruit juices, canned fruit and fruit byproducts.

Disjointed
January 29

Suicide of a transgender teen pleading
Fix society before walking
The path of a truck struck someone remembering

The woman in the portrait, a spirited young American
Full of energy, enthusiasm, determination
My body, able to make a gender violence campaign

Fall victim to crimes at school incidents
Involve crash for cash motor incidents
Involve an induced weather bomb

According to occur when the disturbance happened

Closed early Saturday evening
Workers gave disputed accounts
When Michael Brown met Officer Wilson
A grand jury announced "not inclined to indict"
At a press conference, Nixon called for "peace, respect
and restraint"

In a joint, County Executive Dooley instigated public
safety

Kaitlyn Bolyard

Forgot to Feed the Cat
January 30

As apocalypse authorities worried about zombies
Artificial intelligence like Skynet
They worried about the evil in the world
They had moved to live off the grid
In a veteran RV like third-generation ranchers

They wrote letters to an inmate who slayed in the name
Of God under the banner of Heaven
With a literary reputation conducted at the outer limits
His focus shifted to isolated communities of
fundamentalists
Polygamy in civil establishment, Taliban theocracies and
zealots

In September, in a locked bedroom, all five in the family
Tucked into bed and concluded their probe
Died from drug toxicity - methadone, heroin,
pseudoephedrine
Used in the treatment of mental congestion

They left a goodbye letter, a to-do list,
And a common question: whose turn is it?

Muhammad Survives Satirical Staffers
January 31

A pair of angered publication penchants
Images of might and majesty
Inspired receivers of divine revelation only imparted
To these few, unique prophets
Yahweh had given them His spirit through baptism,
our short study decimated the uncowed

Upped bidding on eBay editions
Top cartoonists ran "Je Suis Charlie" with the caption
"Tout est pardonne" offering forgiveness

I am now "financially independent," given $7,000 per
year
Starting from zero, we assume 6% return
A retirement fund that covers conservative investing

"It is we who forgive, not Muhummad"
L'Assemblée nationale rend hommage aux 17 victimes
Killed in the attack, Charb pictured his fist aloft

Kaitlyn Bolyard

Paying the Rent
February 1

He threw his daughter off a bridge
Joyfully left God's hands reaching
Trusting the Lord to cleanse his questions

Your joy or sorrow for all eternity depends on
Becoming frail, your death coming suddenly
Listen carefully to the nurses, they may suggest
Struggling to sell sandwiches instead

Reshaping goodbye, these big names
Find a way to speak to you
If your sentences are correct

This is my thank you to the world
Not everything is abounding in corn
Trite and mawkishly sentimental
A soap opera for film

Television can teach, not just act
The objective is to record images
Drawn from my museum collection

Fundraising generates additional investment
The Chinese make things people actually want
And spend as little as possible on rent

On non-network channels
February 2

Obama endured great pain to explain
Taliban is not terrorist, the Afghan-based
Organization claimed an attack on contract
A fighter infiltrated security forces

The U.S. spent $65 billion to build details
Refused to buy war rugs with overt designs
For fear they would put off strong Pharisees
They would not acknowledge their faith

Put out of the synagogue, a rabbi
Peeped at mikveh and refused to move
An e-mail sent to congregants encouraged
Energetic and highly musical worship

A passionate audience collaborated quickly
On the toughest ex-wife's new husband
In a syndicated series during the latter half
The 80s were sold to local want ads

Reruns and unusual programming debuted
On non-network channels any who
Mostly crappy where I grew up and watched
Each weekend pass without friends

Kaitlyn Bolyard

Stuck on the Tarmac

February 3

A winter weather system took a dump,
Began its trek east with a blast of arctic air.
The crusty ends, right behind, came hard.
Cuban political prisoners thawed cigars,
Conceived an evolved star, a stunning nebula.
They reshaped the nation's obesity
By starting a flu epidemic.

Three officers flew to Utah after attending the funeral of
A black kitten, 3 months old, who enjoyed chemical
weapons.
A watchdog talked about the Cold War,
Ideological invention, dirty clothes, and a hot idea
Former chief justice Robert issued a formal opinion
Fifty years after the victim was beheaded.

A fierce debate raged within the military because
Soldiers illegally remembered the holocaust.
Do you believe passengers, stuck on the tarmac
For 12 hours, should swim in the Mediterranean Sea?
Western Asia was sentenced to two years for corruption.
The first of Virginia's 72 governors wore a rug on his
head

Echoing Back at You

2016
Choked on the Rain

Kaitlyn Bolyard

Don't Do this Keep Calm Thing
January 2

for Jacqueline

The boogeyman will still attack.
Flying downhill for salted caramel cupcakes,
This thief will clean out
Every twenty - something hot guy.
Great photographers know
The army your husband is in.
Crochet for an entire year,
Or create fashion in three minutes.

Stay awake and aware to see:
Crocodiles and alligators ate stains.
This dog's life farted on an envelope,
Crowning the year with drip,
Exactly as shitty as the average Gatsby
Aggressively clapping.
This blank page library cake
Started out with a kiss
And ended in tickled sinuses.

You were never as focused as
Binge watching a fish tank,
Looking at what the selfies dragged in.
Drive like a grandma, avoiding the switches,
Backward like this.
Act aggressively, throw another brick,
And spend thirty minutes closing Wisconsin.

When You Don't Give a Shit

I'll just say this about Donald Trump
He's been busy already, spiritual friends
I just wish this week was over.
The resistance is led by women and park rangers,
But he always stays true to his words.
True kindness is when someone stands up.

The current objects in my gender-neutral bathroom
Hate no one, no matter how many times
They've listened to Trump's campaign speeches.

Attention students: we have a couple new
Course openings. Scientists and Shia LeBeouf
Will perform open heart surgery on Day 7.

These speeches I cannot improve upon.
I never thought a sentence like this would ever be
Uttered: That is an "alternative fact". What IS that?
Here it is, a real thing that exists, but can we all
Agree the Internet is wrong sometimes?

A man can work out his entire life
And still never look fit. Yet real life
Speaks logically, not fanatically
Everything's better when you don't give a shit.

Kaitlyn Bolyard

When a Smile has an Orgasm
January 11

for Andrea

Sister, your heart lives within mosaic,
But sometimes horoscopes fail and
Play dead to a mobile music library.

Sister, you shouldn't laugh,
But stab someone to make it better.
Real imperfect, flawed and quirky,

Sweet sister serendipity,
You are a heartbreaking whiskey.

Fuck You, Baby
January 13

for Carly

Latch on to feed yourself and
Function under the rationale of Bowie.
Really dig in, entrenched in conflict,
Deliciously, intentionally campy.
Bathe in eyeball discomfort,
Unspelled metal bands lost in shootings.
For your first time, bring a friend to
Muddle through a world of monsters.
Transport the glorious oddball of
Common humanity through music.

You are a woman with
The rights of a gun
Abusing consequences.

Kaitlyn Bolyard

Multiracial Beans End the Game
Feb 18

for Mike

Making a big ice breakup
Affects those around him positively.
An impatient cook with an angry stomach,
He admires weeping, blesses the
Tongue, the marvel of taste.
They say it conflicts with the Bible,
But our cheeks hurt from laughing.

Don't leave me again.

The real question, the only
Devastating thing: At the end of
Everything, the Porkverse crossed
Over with the Burgerverse.
When you're scared shitless,
You could always gift a concession stand.
And when Trump meets Skeletor,
Fifteen percent of atheists will
Make their religion relevant.

I selected you naturally, but
I find your lack of talent... disturbing.

From Distance to Disaster
August 13

We voice our stories, fascinate dead praise.
Nurses vacation with us, blue on the plane.
Luck or fate or God's mulatto tunes
Silence our dinner dates.
February was a full moon shuttered,
Mistaken for a gospel pillow.
This slow transportation, calm and angry,
Breaks up insomnia with
Bear attacks and backyard wrestling.

The day you came,
We snuggled up to your sanctions -
Dab dab dab - and choked on the rain.

Kaitlyn Bolyard

2017
Wondering When

Kaitlyn Bolyard

The Longest Post Ever

I.

Do you believe any human to be subhuman?
I'm legitimately curious, not really trying to start a
debate or anything.
Maybe Nazis are still humans or are they pure evil?
If you defend Nazis and racists go fuck yourself
Only the pertinent man will pass as white
Runaway slaves found freedom. They didn't back out.
Now I seem to be missing some people on my friends list.

P. S. I'm all for toppling statues of historical scum bags

The only thing I find troublesome about taking down
statues is a removal of history
I've tried so many kinds of angry protest
In this world, especially in light of recent events
I'm glad I've missed the news the past few days
These ideas will have me breaking through walls, left,
right and center
It's dangerous to go alone... take this!

I wonder, does Trump ever look at things and say,
 "What have I done?" or is he just that stupid
Friends, I'm gonna tell ya what the soldier told me: if
you're going on a mission
Practice shooting, or maybe we should just impeach him

II.

Somehow injured my tailbone to the point of immobility
It's been 5 years since I dodged the reaper

Also today, I had to call 911 on the way to my doctor's
appointment
Sometimes volcanically angry young women are reduced
to invalids
What would you recommend to a family member with
esophageal cancer... and diabetes....
And heart disease... to help boost the healing process
To start feeling better?

I like knowing that some people will remember me as the
girl who yelled at them for eating
I bought a can opener and found a pic I think I actually
look good in
As a white-passing, multi-racial woman of color, I have
always occupied a very weird space
I am the woman dressed in something that comes above
the knees or elbows
But Im having a Sun King Dragon's Delight to celebrate
surviving
I want watermelons
I asked for a big water with my beer, the waitress did not
disappoint

III.

We ate "hate cake" at a "traditional marriage rally" and
now
Timothy and I have some big news to share with
everyone
We've been building a baby's dresser
When my 10 yr old boy asked for a phone case with the
glitter liquid and pink
I asked him, "Are you sure you want THAT one?"

I'd rather have my child, but by golly, if I gotta give her

up, we're going to make it count
There are few things better than wide-mouthed slobbery
baby kisses

I officially have the apartment to myself for the next
week
Home alone for the next few days
Every pair of socks I own are cleaned, folded, and put
away

IV.

Well son of a fuck man
Who could only grunt, shriek, or scream
America is so gridlocked with fuckery
Going according to plan, we just walked into an ambush
For real though, let's put aside all the terrible shit going
on and realize...
Our demise is just one panic attack away

When something troubles me I'm the type of person who
needs to talk about it
We were both feeling stressed
At twenty-eight, I snitch all the time. Everyone will
know your secrets.
The things we've seen are just so "weird"
I couldn't believe the "truth" until I knew it
myself...WOW

Then we drove through two states
We caravanned to Indianapolis, a day trip to see the
sunflowers
We needed a pilgrimage

V.

Echoing Back at You

Art Garfunkel has a M. A. in mathematics
JFK seldom talked about his sister Rosemary Kennedy,
who was a bubbly champagne
Today's got me thinking about how Harriet Tubman
carried a pistol and how
Kim K said she is naïve about racism

So many things I want to say right now but would make
this the longest post ever

Kaitlyn Bolyard

To My Doorstep

Dear Mr. Postman, when you deliver packages in the
hood
At least try to ring the doorbell
Someone just spent a hundred dollars I no longer have
While I've been working in my own realm

Hey Facebook friends, I give up
I was doing so much better on my own

But this one anxiety med I took didn't work
I'm trying to make a sensory / calm area
I'm procrastinating pretty hard on all the stuff I have to
do
Finally buying into YouTube since this is where I lose
The most tears every day

Doctor, I know I'm starting to gain weight back
Sitting on the porch like a lazy shit
Wondering if anyone has extra bean bags they would like
to donate
I have wanted and have been putting off buying a bike
the last few years
Hundreds of Green Bay families have a meal to come
home to
Thanks to the food pantry, I'm cooking tonight

Our beloved Tilapia passed away last night

So I guess I just get to stay sick because even with my
insurance
The second bout of antibiotics leaves me feeling like
Game of Thrones

Echoing Back at You

Lost and dying from untreated wounds

What did you do during the twenties, Mom?
Happy birthday, Mom. Are you ready to explore the
universe?
Unless you're doing a duckface, this smiling thing really
works
I'm placing my order tomorrow for the anti-plaque /
whitening toothpaste
I'm back from the most wonderful relaxing vacation ever
Each state hilariously depicted by stereotypes

Proud moment: I feel cute as fuck today
And yesterday I felt as confident as someone with an 800
credit score
Might be the post pregnancy hormones
But the generosity of my friends and family has been
delivered

Blow Off Steam after a Long Week

I.

So tired of being an afterthought that my head hurts!
If you ever wanted to buy my love, an SNES Classic
would do nicely.
Thinking of going to the Uptown block party this
afternoon –
Go Band and Go Blue! Not going to mention how humble
I am.
Kapernick and the NFL kneelers now have everyone's
attention,
But it's like beating a dead horse.

II.

Tell me about your favorite picture books to teach
empathy and respect.
Theon Greyjoy killed his fucking dog, let's see who
follows him.
People expecting the world to change overnight are the
same people
That pour KoolAid in the ocean. What's Step 2 of this
plan?
Geek out with mind blowing prints (a sight to see, I tell
ya).
I truly hope everyone finds someone in life that makes
them feel the way
Albert makes me a better person.
Awesomeness met in rainbows before class started today

III.

Echoing Back at You

If you ever shop on Amazon, you need to see this:
Wicket can hardly handle the excitement over his
monthly delivery of fun.
The flash sale was small, but I am super excited that
students showed up
And didn't want to leave.

IV.

I love hearing I don't look 50 years old!
Woot! The day is mine again!
Anyone else going? CCHS Homecoming Weekend
festivities today.
I miss you and expect you to change color like a Mystery
of the Universe.
What is it about me that makes many seemingly sane
women lose their shit?
I know I'm pretty, and I'm a tiger in the sack.
Thanks Katie for being my date – much prefer this to a
hospital bed
I know I've had a long one. Thanks, world, for loving me.

V.

Working all night behind the bar, stop in and try one of
the 62 different beers here.
Labor laws are cool, but mandatory midday work
meetings
Leave me pretty exhausted.
I've pretty much done nothing but school stuff since
Wednesday.
My wit, humor, and joie de vivre can't hurt either.
It was a blast drinking spiced cider in the backyard
while my dude worked

Kaitlyn Bolyard

VI.

Eleven years ago today, I was breaking in the wedding heels
By walking around the house in them while nursing
Fire at my place tonight if anyone is looking.

Incomplete Thoughts

I dreamt of lemon mousse tarts, Lucille Ball
And sweet-hearted redheads, girls I once called friends.
With my warrants paid, I'm finally free and
Pleased to go home in my black velvet dress,
Back to 1996 and memories.

Modern women argue with our dental insurance and
volunteer
For Wisconsin nonprofits, shunning prophets-for-profits.
We take care of things, realizing
Flooding Facebook with chain letters is no kind of
protest.
Us witches craft signs and flaunt ourselves out on the
lawn
In front of white government buildings.

So here's to you, Mrs. Robinson. You live in an
unforgiving place.
Drink wine to forget all the pain, all the laughing.
They fluff your dress, fix your lip gloss,
And as you get sloshed they choose a jukebox tune
You never wanted to listen to.
Later, coherent but cranky, you ask for coffee.

I broadcast my problems on social media,
Seven black and white photos of my life.
The internet explodes my brain with the powers that be.
I pretend this day doesn't exist.
My little sister ain't little no more. She's already
learning
What it means to be.

Stop by and keep me busy.

Kaitlyn Bolyard

Kick me while I'm on the ground already.
How could you ever want to date me?
When I met you, you asked me not to
Go into labor during your anti-bullying presentation.
It just didn't – feel right
But I guess you're not a little boy anymore.

I hope for my future daughter's looks,
She should be beautiful and therefore respected
Able to hold her own at only eight weeks old.
For now, I'll hide in my pillow pile until tomorrow
Wondering when and if my thoughts will ever be
complete.

2018

Dirty Jokes in Verse

Kaitlyn Bolyard

At the Last Intersection
January 15

for Nicholas

Woke up at 9 on Chicago's south side
Making modest sushi, vexed by possessing
Ready for truth in the law of nature
Superior over inferior over superior vexing
Snapped like a reed abducted by death

So happy you agreed to make friends with poets
Who put cinnamon in coffee, make shows of their lives
Winning wager after wager until there is newness
To be wagered with, newness of value

Husband, the biggest issue is what's wrong with this
sentence
This is reality for graduate students, for frontiers of
consciousness,
for sanity and self-preservation wrapped in our own
deaths
What is wrong with this sentence?

Decriminalize and impose a tax to blunder your
plundering
Keep cool and shit, keep shouting for it
Get your baby a fancy booger sucker and look forward to
this
What might be "uncool" with the finger quotes you wrote

Like a Lotioned Glove

January 28

My "more food" face killed any chance at fitness,
Like a new sports bra, supportive but binding.
We ate takeout from a cheap cafe and crafted
Words, composed words in sentences,
Struggled and desired suffering, joy, justice, love,
Abstract concepts like a quick moving virus.
Only mild pain and uneasiness remain.
Which means we can celebrate and maintain
Finding calm ways to party.

I didn't get my eight glasses today.
I'm not diluted enough to think Trump is the most racist
president
But he is codename Penelope and he never goes outside.
Last night he ran, despite the fact he doesn't even like
The colorful world beyond the White House.

I started these new supplements and now
I'm less bloated, I crave water, I take leaps of faith
Off buildings, I get inspired 10 times a day,

I make love and I hunger and I get free Amazon
deliveries.
I feed my face for the children. I worship Americanism.
I eat flavored bath bombs because they just smell so
good.

So I brought my ass out after finding a family member
Unconscious on heroin, resuscitated in Hell.
I will answer any and all questions with a gif.
Feel free to steal this status.
Keep this lazy mama warm and resolve to make 2018

Kaitlyn Bolyard

The year of yoga classes and cute baby pics.

I remember when real love was something I could just
Sink into, like a lotioned glove.

Podcast Psychology
April 8

The worst spelling of my name is Friday.
I go wayfaring in dreams, pick purse enamel
From hate, drain irate parental comments.
A wonderful theme, this time, this art
Born in the wrong era. I won't wear a bra
Or make rainbow chard into old farts.

Wooden wedding notes ruin my honeymoon.
I write fractions as a person to apologize for.
I want the hottest hassle, the biggest bang.
Yes, please, customize my box, eat my munch.
My brain increases negative, stimulates heroic elements,
Super-charged focus for remarkable satisfaction,
Planned and carefully created.

Success is a mind-reaching high on a golden mile,
Rocks dropped on heads headed for splitsville,
A song on a Sunday agenda.
My future self met new friends and took pictures
To prove they exist.

I refuse to clean until weather turns warm, not yet.
This safety net covers your podcast psychology
But won't keep me from getting wet.

Every Piece
May 17

Every piece of us fits together,
Even as we change.
We crown our PMS bitchiness with daisies,
Rings of body fat woven in.
We pay for prime Laurel / Yanny,
Binge our favorite shows and feel like freaks
Getting car sick on the mountains.

There must be a way out of this.
A ha! And a hi-yah! And a kick in the tits!
We need someone to hug us
Without acting like we're asking for attention.
We really need Festivus, an airing of grievances.
We need to help Facebook scientists cure
Our infertility. This is our first time.

Every piece of us fits together.

Our resting bitch faces scare men who catcall.
We take no shit and resign ourselves
To real mad money, finding the perfect age
To make mad money, to stay home on bed rest
Asking friends if they can relate.

Even as we change.

The first time I saw Judge Judy's legs,
She was still in a sitting position,
Pointing to a portion plate,
Telling me what to eat.
So I ate a Hawaiian shirt without a 'stache

Echoing Back at You

And a salesman tried to guilt trip me
When I gave the finger to the corporate fat cats.

Every piece of us fits together,
Even as we change.
Every piece.

Kaitlyn Bolyard

Paid in Trail Mix
May 21

Now I smoke pot with students,
Tell dirty jokes in verse,
Watch fucked up movies that make me
Feel like screaming for free soup.
I host karaoke and enjoy prosperity
Unbruised, skin calloused by time.
My bank got robbed, but this
Bandage will keep the blood from flowing,
And eventually my woman instincts
Will kick in and I'll
Make us some sandwiches

Echoing Back at You

2019

Flashback to the Main Event

The Weirdest Band Name
February 24

Our Trip in the Elevator specializes in statewide Texas pics,
Staying warm on a thirty-degree morning,
Feel-good side eye while listening to the wind.
It's another chili day in Southwest Arizona.
Just finished painting this still-life,
Donut breakfast in church.
It's supposed to be introductory theology, but I'm lost,
Starting to think God and the Devil might be the same person.

This is you. This is you hearing that shit, calling me with 3% battery.
Maybe you'd charge your phone for a job interview but quit playing with me.
To be honest, I love you. You bring me joy.
I get you are in graduate school, but no one wants horribly cooked food
On that little ass stove.
You stay in a one-bedroom and momma can smell weed on everyone's clothes.
We were all having fun and talking. Now you're killing my vibe.
Found an old notebook with two amazing truths in the multiverse.
This is absolutely brilliant. I am speechless.

Here's a pic I took, not Steve Jobs quality, but oh so pretty.
Don't let this ruin your day.
I am interested in R Kelly facing borborygmus, a

rumbling or gurgling made by movement
In the lower intestines, the horrors of socialized
medicine.
When a fool has really stinky breath they always have
something
They really need to tell you.
Flashback to the main event, during my second stay in
Japan,
A tough opponent with bad breath.

Kaitlyn Bolyard

2020

When I Open My Eyes

How dare you call us out like that?
April 4

I'm so disappointed with people's inability to think for
themselves
Why is our generation so unhappy?
Been trying to explain this to some people

How was philosopher ever a job?
I can explain it to you, but I can't understand it for you
When you hate people, I don't judge

After this plague is over, I will sleep
If only past me knew how hard sleeping would become
At first this quarantine thing was enough to make me
want to pull my hair out
I will not take my medical advice from someone without
a board-certified Ph. D.

Woke up to find 4 more friends lost family
I'm no Van Gogh, ladies and gentlemen
But I fully embrace the peace solidarity brings

I Used to Love the Zoo
April 10

Sorry to interrupt your scrolling
To cultivate kind and calm conversations.
I never do these so be gentle.

Quality time is a choice – are you looking to make
someone's day?
I'm hoping for good news soon.
From a grocery store manager:
I'm an okay cook, but
Instead of using buns, I made a homemade big mac
salad.
How many tacos can I get with my $1200 stimulus
check?
My favorite chicken restaurant is representing the best
in humanity during this Covid-19 pandemic.
My favorite food, which I asked for, made a run with my
grill.
I really hope Drekker comes out with a new beer called
Skunky Piss Water
Chonk and Brains... sold half a case

Finally!
It's time to announce the lovely ladies that will be
gracing the Vintage Torque Fest 2020
Who has had a best friend for longer than 7 years?
There's a few that I've been in more contact with lately.
Thousands of t-shirts
For all of us who have been using Vine quotes even
though Vine has been dead for years
Don't hoard during this sale.
We are sorry to announce we will stop producing

clothing.
I guess now we're all living in those old paintings of
people lying around on couches doing nothing with their
boobs out

Why is there a pentagram on your floor?
I'm writing a covid19 nursery rhyme for kids to creepily
sing
Hang in there, Wisconsin!
Keep. It. Up.
Do this without fibbing
It begins again...
I use petroleum jelly at night with a pair of mittens to
keep them moisturized.
Wild bee: getting snack
Me: no prob bee

2020 B. C.
I miss people

When you're bummed its cold today and remember its
cold today...
I can finally smoke my cheese!

If e. e. cummings had Twitter
April 11

Me. Every damn time.
Forgive me, I feel it again
So much nostalgia but with some great upgrades
Quarantine Day 6 and we're all quietly reading
improving books.
This brand-new game is taking word play to a hilarious
new level
Still fun
You like free, right?
Lady Gaga literally put her money where her mouth is
Y'all having me check my bank account every 5 mins

Even this cat knows how to social distance
During a mask shortage
Dog: do you really expect me to make pancakes with
paws?
30 adorable beavers to celebrate National Beaver Day
Love Ryan Reynolds.
Men need to understand that not all women are the
same
I have to remind him to get me cilantro
I'm heartbroken, but I understand
Themed boxes for people who give a damn
Since Easter is soon, here's a friendly reminder
I'm watching you

Up having my quarantine coffee and a discussion with
my lovely wife
Hey board game friends
The only type of friends I allow in my life
Heard dumb funny thing

Kaitlyn Bolyard

What day is it?
Stay the f*ck home forever!
I'm going to the store

But if I lay here, if I just lay here
This will be a wonderful day
I mean, look at what I've accomplished
I'm all about juice and safety
Is anyone aware of cookie decorating kits at the local
bakers?
Todays rushed takeout from an empty café
When it's finally your turn to enter the grocery store
Unnecessary things people waste money on

I hope my boyfriend knows that even when things aren't
going right
I'll settle for a hair sniffer over an unapologetic pussy
grabber

sobbing my 11 year old just asked me to play my 80's
playlist by saying
"mama can we hear those weird songs from the nineteen
hundreds?"

Help out by walking back and forth between my
keyboard and monitor
I'm silently correcting your grammar
Prepare for the ultimate gaslighting
When Covid19 enters my body and sees how it's running
on nothing
But caffeine and anxiety

7 Surprising Truths
April 13

Been a stressful up and down day today
A pregnant woman gets out of her room and goes to the
fridge
Makes amazing changes on the way

They made me a sign
Snapped a close-up object
Anyone know anyone that picks up scrap metal?
This is the dream

Listen, am I the most attractive girl out there?
Yep, still learning this
Sometimes decadence is its own reward

Pick your quarantine house
Netflix, weighted blanket, pantry full of snacks
Tensions are high in the produce section

Of course, I'm glad for this outcome
Bibimbap cooked for me by my lovely daughter
Which red jacket would you pick
In honor of this year's class of 2020 seniors?
Nice try, Mario

After "supervising" me this morning, Mulan decided to
be lazy
This will be me, no doubt in my mind
Those of you saying things like, "If you don't like Trump,
don't take his money,"
Please understand:
I found patient zero, but

Kaitlyn Bolyard

Not one doctor for grandma

I want somebody to stand up at my funeral and say
Damn Bellatrix, let's just be racist real loud in a quiet
room, why don't we?

Who is Responsible for this Fuckery?
April 18

I have survived coronavirus by social distancing
Wearing a mask over my ugly face since 1978
Quarantine cookies motivate me to find
A good local sub shop that's open, to eat
A big ole satchel of Richards and
Pick up my to-go beer, feeling frosty
And delicious ordering delivery

So many people ready to be Rambo now,
Even my husband who DJed
Every possible shade, a Memphis shuffle
On a hot summer day, this style
Listening to three bands on replay

Protestors of Gov. Ever's 'Safer at Home' extension
Met up at the mall, mentioning Wisconsin
In a nod to dairy farmers on TV, but what
Do they have to liberate but their sex lives?
Barely alive on what is it? Day 365?

Happy birthday to my 16-year-old
Excusing herself from homework group today
Posting her tits before digging through
Boxes we haven't unpacked yet

Self-care is also narrating your story
Finding your stash in this
Existence

You're Bored, Too

April 21

Do you know how Jeep owners drive past one another?
Let's protest COVID-19 stay at home orders!
Yeah, if they cancel football, I'm kicking somebody's ass!
So, you guys are now pro-choice?

Due to less pollution, the latitudes and longitudes are
now visible in the sky
This social distancing is no big deal 'cause no one likes
me anyway
I like being at home in my own little world, eating
Japanese snacks
I'm finding that acquiring a sleeveless denim jacket is
harder than one might imagine
Anyone else frustrated with incompetency?

Today I made a mask from an old fave t-shirt
To hide my resting bitch face
This should be played at full volume, preferably in a
residential area
Extrovert level: high
If I can't avoid a covid of some kind, this will do

Tool are hoping to make a new EP while in quarantine
The first 4 people that comment on this post will receive
from me
My favorite craft beers and an Oedipal complex.
Do the thing because you're bored, too.

Welcome to the Shitshow
April 24

Now we make essential garbage disposals
For assholes in Kenosha, Covid cases at almost 300.
I guess it needs to be said:
Those guys who are protesting have been
Dreaming of an apocalypse their whole lives,
Would rather wake up screaming than dead.

I met a man on the London bridge and asked
Had he ever been a Doctor of the Who variety.
I saw an oddball with hyper specific interests
Share their color depositing conditioner,
This rare combination of tornado and rainbow.
A being of the dark shadows saw someone sad,
Projected movies on the Smile, It's Friday,
Eating cake amid cacophony.

I'm curious to know who can actually say they have a
High school diploma and no felonies.
Anyone can be stupid enough to be President these days.
I'm surviving quarantine life,
Staying woke and healthy, but
I miss people and as summer arrives,
Do we just cut the legs off our pajamas?
Spent time in nature, starting a garden balcony,
Watching all of Cheers and then all of Frasier.

Kaitlyn Bolyard

Dear Non-Essential Employees
April 30

Don't get excited over the mail
Over the IRS
Over the armed men storming Michigan
Maybe Trump is the president we deserve

Heads up Kenosha and Racine peeps,
If you love someone, be happy as the sun
Learn to enjoy the rain as much

Hey vagina people,
Spread equality, not germs
Dreamed I was a muffler last night, not a whore
Take care of yourself, like you did before

My son misses his D&D group at the local gaming store,
Digital board games, counting pencils,
Gifts for my first set of babies
So, should I send my bill to the teacher for doing her job?
Feeling nostalgic for nosebleeds

To my friends working from home,
Get used to answering, "Where'd you get that?"
Take a hike straight to the waterfall
Without revealing your age.

Light Pink Girl, Texting
May 1

Was it worth meeting me?
I miss elves, warlocks, even stand-up comedians
Helping me enjoy my life, can't lie.
Anxiety makes me feel trapped, worried about the world.
Tried a menstrual disk offering 12 hours of worry-free
protection,
But it didn't work. The more you know.

New beer alert: Hippy's wife
Staying true for over 10 years with her
Art therapy life coach certification.
Drink it alongside pizza of the month,
Avoiding chicken, nearly 900 Tyson workers tested
positive.

Show me your favorite tattoo, the theme song
Playing every time you enter a room. Make me happy.
Becky is just a younger Karen,
Wanting more than anything to be part of the gang.
How long do we have to catch up to the U.K.?

North by Northwest, measured in pencils.
Help fill my creative sails,
Enjoying some patio time,
Taking 2.5 seconds to text "hi."

Kaitlyn Bolyard

Say Insulting Things and Pretend
May 30

When is Aldi getting window units
So I can seal away summer?
Monarchs lay their eggs in the eaves
Searching for a sunshine adventure
When all I can feel is the heat.
I'm not sure why it hit like it did.
Transform your skin with helpful actions.

Afterall, the council voted down the face mask
requirement,
So now we can spot beauties at the MGM Grand
Before chopping our hair off in solidarity.

He looted a Lego death star set
Before sentencing one of my baby foxes to murder
By roadside fuel jets. I wonder how many points he
would get
If he used Mortal Kombat rules instead.

So this is why black lives matter,
Why anger runneth over.
Speak up, they said, but protest peacefully
Without saying a word.

We run a bot that crawls the web,
Sooner than you can say 'welcome' with a
Well-thought-out sign.
The silent king returns
To awaken his sleeping mummies.

Without further ado, I introduce to you
A fun drinking game.

Echoing Back at You

Say insulting things and pretend
The bartender can't hear you.

Kaitlyn Bolyard

The First Time in a Long Time
June 1

This year will be written in history,
Every month in 2020,
Every sad week for America.
How old were you when you realized
Just how much we suck?
What if I told you there was a way
To remove your years of tattoos,
To crack your entire body like a glow stick?
To see the last, full strawberry moon?

He turned out the lights and hid in his bunker.
Strong man with little hands threatens to violate
Free speech, won't hear a word against him.
Shameful in his own dreams.

Milwaukee goes nuts again
As a cop removes his colleague's knee.
Showcasing for the people outside the U.S.
How compassionate we can be.
When someone claims "not all cops are evil"
Protests erupt in Kenosha, and we ask
Where do you stand?
I am a rifle waiting for someone to point and aim,
But which side will claim me?

A small percentage of looting rioters -
Bullshit rioting -
Posts about protesters looting.
What really matters is
None of us can breathe.

If you know someone in isolation,

Echoing Back at You

If you are interested in change,
If your life is never fucking normal
It never will be.

This is the first time in a long time
I've died on the inside.

Kaitlyn Bolyard

Too Perfect to Distort
December 17

I'm looking to get away from chemical syrup,
Relive 10 years of Facebook memories.
We spent our morning doing Peppa's favorite things -
It was a short list.
The temp got above 35 degrees, just for fun.
I don't know shit about horoscopes or crystals,
But your age is equal to the number of cartoons you've
watched.
Today I'm only 21.

If there's a god, He's into gingers, but he also invented
depression.
Fucking awful depression.
I'm looking for a good dermatologist – it's a sad day for
zits.
The best gift ever, from our family to yours -
CBS all access, chilly under the blankets.

A new study recently found we should
Study words of the past, but I'm not sure
If we've missed them enough yet.

I've found guys so cute I didn't want to eat them,
Their faces just too perfect to distort.

I Want to See a New Year
December 37

Wear your mask in Washington if you need help.
Make sure it covers your whole face, your whole goddam race.
This is a really strange way to learn cops know how to hold fire.
That they know their colors all too well.
They would never need paint-by-number instructions,
Just leave the canvas blank, white as an untouched witness.

We tell them you lost, get over it,
But I still need my safe spaces, my emotional support pizza.
Stuffing my face while wondering
How anyone is surprised by what happened today.
How 82-year-old hands that used to pick somebody else's cotton
Could ever be entirely forgotten.
Like they'd never seen a human being with black skin.

Maybe they couldn't reinforce the barrier,
The walls weren't high enough to protect them,
But every time they turn off a body camera, or worse don't have one,
It should come with an automatic charge of destroying evidence.

To the so-called Patriots,
You are a lying sack of shit with nothing to wear
Claim you stand head-to-toe wearing God's armor
But you'd even cuss out a food bank volunteer.

Kaitlyn Bolyard

We're not asking you to shoot them like you shoot us,
But
Given that it's only January
Part of me is hoping this isn't real.
That this dishonor has not come upon our family.
The American People haven't aged well
In this stupid cringe-ass country.
I never thought former President George W. Bush would
look so good,
Or sound so smart, comparing us to a Banana Republic.
Momentarily forgetting his hatred of Muslims.

I used to think I could lift anything, for I am strong.
But my strength is slowly cracking, and I turn to humor
In an effort to not entirely fall apart.
After all, it's only a coup if it's from the coup d'état
region.
This is just sparkling white supremacy.
It's just the hue difference between a protest and a riot.

What we have all seen today, in our nation's capitol,
Is what you get when you order Night at the Museum
from Wish.
Black lives still matter.
The ghetto still exists.
When civil rights organizations call out the President,
When the President clandestinely plots to overthrow a
government.
There is no vaccine to protect us from this illness.

And if you are a giver, know your limits.
Stop hate but also bear witness because
The wrong things will always catch your attention.
Don't yes yourself to death
May your choices reflect your hopes, not your fears.
Maybe living through those petty days will get us

through this danger,
Help us draft articles of impeachment,
But this week has been a parade of horrors.
We must protect our mental health.
To make it here without dying is the epitome of white
privilege.
Maybe a blind Justice could answer our questions,
Could conjure the magic of hope again,
To make us be and do better.

Every year, we plan for a happier January,
Plan to improve ourselves, our society.
We must never stop believing
Beautiful things can happen, even in times of chaos.
The U.S. capital has not been breached since the war of
1812.
History will rightly remember today's violence,
Republicans in congress cowering under their desks.
Damn, I'm tired of living through these historical events.

America owes itself an apology.
We want to blame the behavior, but there is clearly
A systemic problem here.
What happened today was an insurrection.
No government will ever announce it's become a police
state.

Mining social media for my own mental health,
Digging through these shenanigans until I get grounded
from Twitter
For guillotining the President.
And if this gets me suspended from all social media
For calling out the greatest domestic terrorist threat
A threat to our democracy, brace yourself for the latest
conspiracy.

Kaitlyn Bolyard

Shout out to all my people.
When I open my eyes, I want to see something happy.

I want to see a new year.

Echoing Back at You

2021

A Primal Sort of Self Care

Kaitlyn Bolyard

The Package You Forgot You Ordered

January 2

I have enough on my to-do list
Without this weird headache,
Without this smoke in my eyes.

People of Earth,
I am shocked at how many of you
Have become door mats.
Why aren't you mad?

I studied this killer in my college psychology class,
He danced like my dad, drunk and awkward.

It's good to be weird, but not when you're looking
For an apartment to rent. You have to hide
So many parts of yourself to fit in.

This is so true: we neglect to take care of mental health,
Forget about online therapy.
Some scientists are especially worried about this.
It's too smart for my brain, hurts to connect
Through wires and constructs,
Through zoom meetings, feeling alone in a Brady Bunch
Show opening, so I watch videos, dream of a
Road trip cross-country, no cares in the world,
Wind blowing through my hair.

Instead, I cover my head and brave another snowstorm.
Thought about trying a sober February
Until I found whiskey-flavored Listerine
And a savage trombone player to meet my needs.

What's something you'd do if you didn't have kids? I
asked.

Echoing Back at You

Open this umbrella in your musty butthole, she said.
Not the response I was expecting. But she's weird, at
least.

Books are proof humans can do magic, that
More poetry is needed, so I'm back at it.
Did you know, after all I've done for you,
You're not alone? You've upgraded,
And the package you forgot you ordered
Has arrived on the doorstep.

Believing in Absurdities
January 13

Got a great video game idea
But literature is the most agreeable way of ignoring life.
Tomorrow I'm off work for a rare moment,
A too-good-to-be-true moment.
Giving y'all freedom of speech,
Freedom to say yes, I love my wife.
Tonight, we snuggled, went to sleep,
Shared good things about 2020 and started
Day 6 of decluttering.
Gossiped in the kitchen while I reported my uncle to the
FBI
For the massive crack in the Antarctic.

If you treat your dog like a human child,
Tell him why he can't have more snacks.
Tell him God said no.
Take a post lunch walk, then nap with puppies.
If I earned it, I drink in a neutral milk hotel
Have a wild Saturday night,
Add you like an attachment.
My best makeup looks make for a fabulous day.
These styles are officially off limits.

Every Republican today screaming about "censorship"
Should hear my favorite country song
Then watch VFW. Read an entirely redacted document.

Lot of y'all was out on New Year's,
Fogging up glasses,
Swapping comfy for cute,
Remembering 1974 like

Echoing Back at You

You want so much to be anywhere but here.
Deadheads in my journal,
Noticing terrifying thoughts and self-sabotage.
Wishing for salon-quality results,
To be the first person tonight.

Other moms never forget this
In slo-mo attack mode, counterintuitive.
Instead of flying for an hour,
Get knotty knickers during your Clayton Bigsby
sighting.
Light winter forest campfires.
Then worship the Full Metal Octopus.

My sweet boy lost his fight, just a dog
Challenging ducks, stretching,
Believing in absurdities.

Like a French Girl
January 19

No matter what your V-day plans are,
You should draw me like a French girl
In the Cayman Islands, just spend the day
Walking in a ski mask in the snow,
Kick-starting an epic adventure
An imaginary fuckery of executive dysfunction.

Go through stuff like Monday motivation
Through things stuffed in the closet at your mom's house
Throwing insults like OK, fuckers, you go first,
Before trying endless masturbatory combinations.
You know, you can cook a chicken with kinetic energy
By slapping it and naming it Elizabeth. That's some
special skin care.

Kaitlyn Bolyard

There are at least five foundational principles
To a thriving polyamorous woman, to the new
Female Vice President with something to say.
Sugaring is two times quicker, but I'm grateful for medications,
And my hubby's home state, his current mood.

Books are no more threatened by Kindle than stairs are by elevators,
But when Merry and Pippin have a disagreement, they force
Premature selling out.
Crone status should be embraced.
Not sure how we made it, but this is a gift.
Do you have any thoughts? How about prayers?

Do you ever wonder how much sawdust
You can put in a rice crispy treat before they notice?
Y'all mad a woman is shot dead storming a Capitol building
But there's been sightings of a dragon,
There've been reasons for a female to be found,
To be thrifty, to make 2021 an amazing start,
To be the reason cam hams wanna see some.

Would any of my friends call themselves a bully,
Carry symptoms of Crohn's disease in their bellies
Build a wall around every meal kit they've found
Like New Age witches cursing home?

I told you guys… I'm losing it
Over your brother loving me in the DMs,
Shoveling colds and COVID like heavy snow.
I'd rather just blush and go home. Read a book.
Play with dark, scary colors on my computer.
Shaking the day through dice and stop paying

Echoing Back at You

For clothes, start taking precalculus,
Binge watching the original muppet show.

So tell me, did that POS finally step down?
Did he make it to Sesame Street?
Many people, myself included,
Teach far better from home than dead.
Is there a historical precedent to reflect
On this contemporary moment?

If you played, what kind of vibe would I give off?
In what role would you cast me?
I still think you should draw me.

Kaitlyn Bolyard

Starting something new with a chef's kiss
January 20

Anyone know what is going on?
Do you kind of love this as much as me?
I've been working with a financial advisor,
Saving pennies in a bottle for special occasions,
And I finally got to watch the whole inauguration.
I abuse dark humor to get me through,
Express myself through writing.
I don't mean to brag, but I think we all agree,
Poetry was the best part.
No hipster posers, please.

I never knew we'd yearn for hungry roots,
The pigtail mafia, sleepy and so big,
Shea butter and avocado on freshly shaved legs.
I was incredibly nervous about my first class back to
school,
Evaluating zoom tendencies and my couch situation.
How about all of you just live your own lives,
Stop judging the weight I've worn my entire adult life.
Start asking who the fuck closed last night
And abandon country music to read a few pages.

Hands down, my new favorite Paris climate agreement
Invites Michelle Obama to go back to living like we did,
With strong women guessing what works for their skin,
Trying new recipes for slapped chicken.
But in the end, America chose the boy with the stutter
Over the bully, an easy orange mark
For different shades of pigment.
Can we all let out a collective
Sigh of relief? Drench ourselves in serotonin?

Echoing Back at You

This is what we needed.

I also need this Bernie Sanders moment
To become the new "I don't want to" stand in.
Nobody working 40 hours a week should be in poverty.
Keep the memes coming. I said,
Get in mothafucker, and the internet is weird,
Crossdressing style resolutions with news updates
Slaying until I'm dead and somehow that's a good thing.

My dog yoinked the crap outta those toys
And I figure what works for him
Might make me happy, too.
If one house plant makes me smile,
What about a whole garden?
What about a day with no shoes?
A student's tooth fell out and got lost among
The inauguration day celebrations as we
Added to our many, many pet snuggle pics.
You're not mad that someone else might soon make $15
an hour
Or wear trendy sustainable earrings,
You want to stay hopeful with whole family chats,
Swallow your feelings, hail to the chief on a new
frequency.

Under new management, maybe fewer of my friends will
die.
If you've ever been the only, the first, or one of the few,
Take your chance for a crime of opportunity.
We all need a "feel good moment."

I am not sorry for watching mesmerized as a functional
government
Watches skinny black girls out for a ride without

catcalling
Or creating an objectified birthday expectation at
bedtime.
Anyone know a reliable world,
A space where I can wait on a crock pot,
In a brighter place? She told us
There is always light, if only we're brave enough to see it.
If only salon quality results came direct
From customer complaints, I'd glow for sure.

Opening Argument
February 10

I will die next to a pile of books I planned to read
At the southwest corner of 56th St and 7th Ave, circa
1925.
My therapist told me to get specific, but maybe not
specific about my death.
Right now, I'm a little nervous.

Pushing out the back door, full of fiery hate for Joss
Whedon,
And that lady making nachos on the countertop with her
hands.
In both cases, I'll pass on that invite, I'd rather color my
hair
As a stop-gap to breakdown, reminding myself of the
little black book
I used to have, that exciting, terrifying manic daydream.
Only some of you truly understand the moisture I
sometimes need.
Those stripper poles really do deserve a break.

The Republican party tent can't handle me, wouldn't
want me in any case.
Voters in Kenosha and Racine won't wear two masks,
won't even wear one,
Would rather cause police scenes at Menards with their
naked noses.
Please, spread the word, not the herd immunity here,
Lighting up legalized marijuana, just chill.

I feel so threatened by your great books, not your love of
reading.

Kaitlyn Bolyard

My new full-time job is wire-wrapping user personas for
content strategy,
Mumbling through biracial technologies, wire-tapping
Trump's second impeachment hearing overrun by the
super bowl.

I remind myself it's okay to not do it all today,
To just take a piece of it, a moment, a pause.
Stop to think, before beginning an opening argument.

Wish for Something Better
May 31

Tomorrow is the day I start my push-up challenge.
Not today, today is too heavy, today I'm too heavy.

My man touched my leg, examined the halo over my
head.
I realize now my hair can be great if I never expect it to
be straight
And if I'm the kind of wife who never cheats on her
husband.

My least favorite conversation starter as a parent,
Mom I have something I need to tell you.
Now only God can help us because our feet are the same
size.
I tried to have a normal conversation, but he just
Wished me a happy birthday. I never want a birthday
again.

In fact, I've been feeling really low, so down and over it.
My anxiety can't handle going outside,
Going through life like I don't know how to live, what to
do.
A partygoer tested positive for COVID-19, but by now
That's old news. I've always been the weird one in the
group,
Begging my way to amazing Indian food.
Drove to Manitowoc for cheeseburgers and now I want to
know
Which in-town breakfast joints offer carry out.

Kaitlyn Bolyard

In real news, white supremacist agitators want protest
chaos.
I'm an observer, but even I can't watch.
I understand that I will never understand.
I've never burned a building, never watched one burn,
Felt the flames licking up around my face.

I have a pretty good network in Minnesota and when
People started rioting, I knew America was a tinderbox
Ready to alight and explode with the right intonation.

Black lives matter. Black lives matter.

If its safe to mail tax refunds, its safe for me to write
poetry,
To write a big long thing, but I don't know what to say,
Except happy birthday, mom, blow out the candles
And wish for something better than this.

Masquerading as Wisdom
July 8

The topic is comics, blogs beginning with talking shit,
Becoming friends, taking nerdiness and cat ownership
To next-level madness. Becoming version 2.0,
In dire need of a vampire heist film,
Stealing cursed objects d'art.

Your body is 70% water and I'm thirsty
For chocolate.

We build a common language, deliberate and powerful,
Love writing our words on all available surfaces,
Using any and all desirable pronouns.
If someone says you're "complicated," they disrespect
your pride,
Hide their real emotions in black-and-white,
Shadows of the real people they used to be,
People with actual thoughts and feelings,
Comfortable in gray haze.

Give me your dread, your suffering, your rage,
And I will make something beautiful,
A collage of your mutterings.

The post-partum fears of my body are settling in,
This extra space no longer supporting a life
Other than my own.
I have these creepy feelings encroaching on what
Society says should happen.

The only baby I will birth will be these creations,

Kaitlyn Bolyard

These machinations of nonce masquerading as wisdom.

Too Punk to Survive
July 16

Save these foreskin style tips for Twin Lakes, Wisconsin,
Country Thunder needs more lightning, I think,
More brazen animosity for out-of-office nonsense.
What decadence that "vanilla" means plain,
That a $900 sofa doesn't sound insane.

Burrito or pasta, I no longer play that game,
Instead salad, salad, salad, maybe a chicken breast
Pretending to be sexy, offer words of encouragement,
In a limited number of characters,
Social media wisdom to reach my ideal weight.
Wouldn't it be great if we all grew a different crop,
Met up to trade, and just ate for free?
But even dirt has a price, as does U.S. history.
God listening in, judging all of us crazy,
Ripping our hearts to shreds,
Stomping on the ground as we drown.

I love reading at night, before sleep comes to me,
In the between time,
Like a baby duck marveling at existence.
My mother uses her Kindle as a bookmark in a
paperback.

I once thought I had slept a month,
Woke with the nurse leaning over me,
Keeping the doctor from killing me each morning.
The further down you scroll, the higher I get.

The Amazon driver left the porch door open,
Releasing kitten to the wild unknown, a new land
For survival, an outlaw scent matching his personality.

Kaitlyn Bolyard

We could use a few volunteers to rescue his whiskers.
Canadians look both ways when they see miles per hour
Instead of syrup per moose.
Somewhere, a tree remembers you because it enjoyed
your company,
Writing a fiction story while skating the frozen pond,
Me, freezing, dumping laundry on the bed, naked and
shivering,
Learning the importance of vaccines from Oregon Trail,
Black and green in the night.

Feeling crazy about dieting, trying to embrace the real
me,
My size, my thighs, my everything,
Embracing the most challenging relationship, with
myself,
Feeling too toxic, too punk to survive.

And So Can We

August 1

Already August, so here's an update on my summer,
How my childhood punishments have become adult
goals.
How I struggle through vision boards and
communicating
With certain people, with free advice.
Went sailing last night, with a verse in my heart,
dreaming of homeownership –
Things that were a given just a generation ago.

This is dedicated to all those who didn't believe in me,
In free universal healthcare,
In my ability to make medical decisions about my own
body,
This flesh vessel carrying my thoughts and dreams,
The only thing I thought was truly mine but turns out I
don't own it, either.
Not even anything I produce, really.

Friends come in all shapes and sizes, in memorial photos
trying to capture souls,
Trying to hold them a moment longer, to tie them to
heartstrings,
Thread them to our seams. I would cry (happy tears) if
we could just
Be together again in our brokenness, incomplete.
Somehow this golden age doesn't need to be perfect, just
united,
Supporting locally, learning rules so we can break them
delicately,
Stealing so subtly you won't even notice what's missing.

Kaitlyn Bolyard

If Simone could win Nationals with broken toes in both
her feet,
I think she can take a rest when she needs one,

And so can we.

My Death Sentence

August 17

Trimmed my beard while wearing a mask today.
I don't remember what my lips even look like.
What these personally curated essential oils smell like:
Patchouli, vanilla, eu de social distancing,
Haven't worn deodorant since last May, anyway.

I rocked the boat while we were still afloat,
Swirled my fingers in swaying waves,
Learned the meaning of "personal growth"
Let my armpits breathe and fungal feet breed psoriasis.

Had another delightful birthday alone, wishing for
Customized skincare and catered colognes,
Ready-to-wear radishes, something new I think you'll
like.

My town has turned into a detective experience,
Not sure where construction begins and failing
businesses end.
I never knew we had so many resident scientists,
Micro-dosing on each hypothesis, researching nonsense.

My dog still has the best life, doesn't understand what
I'm
Struggling with, what I'm up against. He thinks relaxing
should be
My top priority – I agree with him a thousand percent.
But just because I behave ridiculous on the internet,
Doesn't mean I wear these stripes in real life.

I know you're in pain, wanted to smoke sausage today,

Kaitlyn Bolyard

But storms rolled in again, and your Fall plans
Have been derailed by the Delta variant,
And I requested a last meal of chicken nuggets
Before they carry out my death sentence.

Long Boi's Shadowy Release
August 24

Fresh cut grass, plants and rain
Scent of stripper skid-marked on my sweat
Ginger-colored moments, slowing, breathing
Feel like crotch goblins need to vacate this premises
There is never any feeling good with this insatiable
Long Boi

You take control, chugging cottage cheese with ease
Like these rich, gross pay cuts, pay taxes no heed
Testing each porn site for compliance, researching the
diseased
Been chasing other people's dreams so long
You misplaced your notes again

Used to like radio but they destroy each song,
Charge a standard shipping fee for each
Yesterday, tomorrow and today, even stressing
"Sound on", like Long Boi's hotdog is basically pureed
meat stuffed inside
An animal casing, lost your Sunday chill

I'd like to think that those older than me would be more
mature,
But we each have more marbles for emergencies
And my trauma doesn't negate your trauma
Between breathing, we ask ourselves serious questions,
Between breathing

I create with you a common goal,
An entire Picasso, a faded Roddenberry,
But the problem with solar is we can't monopolize the
sun

Kaitlyn Bolyard

And Long Boi prefers a shadowy release.

Join the Crew
September 5

Growing conscious, classist entrepreneurs
Starting with daddy's money and selling products,
moving money
Well spent, moving money should redistribute across
Google maps, 30 minutes before the turn of civilization.

Time is sacred in Mexico, as dogs walk down parades
and the pope,
Boring as ever, does one small thing for a million thank
yous,
All those intercessory prayers, sending up our thoughts
to the clouds.
When we're starving, they just want to take a picture.

Research styles on sale, unseen progress.
Unleash your inner animal. What my back needs is a
saddle
So I can be more useful, become a new absolutely
ridiculous mascot.
Laugh as much as you breathe. Always fresh, always
fun,
Always your birthday.

Do you ever forget to hide your expressions, hide your
abortions,
Hide your highly rated litter-robot in the corner of your
mind?
So weird to see them recruiting students, rehearsing,
Like they know what our parents were talking about,
Like they know the crew.

Kaitlyn Bolyard

Transforming Tears into Bullets

Y'all better respect CNAs, academics absorbing
knowledge,
Sustainable, soulless office jobs we now wish we had
Along with work/life balance. I want to read
A book explaining what really happened,
Try out a new mind-mapping tool to understand.

Please read the below press release,
An update regarding a missing adult from Gurnee,
The full-page countdown to celebrity fuck-ability,
Moving beyond the flirtatious period to outright child
porn.

When was the exact moment you realized
Humans weren't gonna make it as a species?
These tweets can be rough to read.
Hasn't been my hour, my day, my week.

A concerned citizen drove past my residence,
Worried about how comfortable I am in my skin,
Just my skin, and I can't afford curtains yet.
We told ourselves we'd be more positive,
Reduce our sound sensitivities, activate
Camouflage mode, just survive.
It seemed sketch, even then.

I wonder what my parents at my age
Worried about. Surely not something like
Bodily autonomy. How to afford dinner and a movie.
How to cultivate kind and calm conversations and
Harvest cemetery honey. Surely,
They didn't transform their tears into bullets.

When I Forget to Wish Her

September 20

'Till death she will be the death of me.
Progenitor of midnight tear-filled calls.
I want to be a matriarch, say exactly what's on my mind,
Demand Oxford commas and Gottman Couples Therapy,
But she... she will always be my design.
Made in my image, albeit not intentionally,
Always hip, always happening,
A scene all her own, infected by hereditary genes.

So, I missed another milestone, another chance.
There's not enough room for this heart stabbing.
I'm officially open for available therapists challenging
My already heavy haul this year.
My least favorite reminder of what should be fun,
Always leaving breadcrumbs behind for future tenants,
Thirsty house plants, nightmares strung between
Roller coasters and goat man torsos.

My daughter, seven as of yesterday, causes me the worst
mom guilt,
Especially on her birthday, when I forget to wish her
happy.

What's It All Worth, Anyway?
September 23

Some lucky waiters are paid to be rude to you.
An awakening, that role reversal, uncomfortably
obscene.

We believe parents should provide first and last month's
rent
Along with everyday essentials, don't just shove your son
Out of the nest like that, he's not ready. We're not ready
to face
The world, dazed and confused. We're not ready for the
interview.

The unnerving, unasked and unanswered questions left
in our obituaries –
How do you measure a life, after all, which details
matter?
Who cares where we worked, if we procreated, who
survives us?
Did we spend hours on the train, contemplating
philosophy,
Meditating on the existence of god? Staring into the
void?

Apparently, we can find the answers in genetic testing,
Imprinted on our DNA. Our ancestors have been there
And we only exist to repeat, before and after,
Their memories. The results are ordinary,
Wasted time every evening, repeating.
The small business of asking.
Pretending Bukowski said something deep.

We start making therapy second-nature, easy,

Echoing Back at You

Taking each stupid moment and summing it up in
medication.
Just when you think you've got it figured out, you blink,
And the destination moves farther away, slightly
electrified,
Like the world's best forked wall socket.
Not a suicide attempt, but a scream for attention,
A toilet-paper napkin held out like rations,
Each dollar doled out to street beggars,
Or, more often, anxiously withheld.

Fidgeting, but Surviving
September 24

Put in two weeks at the last warehouse job I'll ever have,
Never going back, I swear it, though I worked at Amazon
twice,
Third shift for a wage increase, inflated, not even worth
it,
Not allowed to clock in early but expected anyway.
I have an idea: Let's not ever go back.

Every time I get groceries, I am amazed at how little $20
can buy,
Remember times when food pantries provided
sustenance,
Me, a single, broke white woman suddenly burdened
with almost
Forty pounds of frozen chicken and mostly rotten
produce,
A year's supply of cranberry sauce.
My meals dictated by whatever canned goods people
pulled from
Dusty back cupboards to donate.

I've decided that from here on out if anyone tries to judge
me
Based on my history, I will remember the struggle,
Remind myself I've lived through worse,
Can do it again if I need to. I won't miss out on one
moment,
Just remember how it used to be.

How we ate cherry-flavored lollipops that tasted like
cough syrup,

Echoing Back at You

How you got me to come over with the promise of Jolly
Rancher vodka.
How I tried smoking, swallowing, tripping, but never
cocaine.
Back when we paid long distance charges to call one
town over,
And didn't bother waiting for Friday.

I haven't forgotten how to socialize, but often retreat into
myself,
Stay safe in bed with a book instead, go to bed on time.
This year itself has been so ridiculous and weird, that I
Like everyone else, am just coping, not surprised
anymore.
I wear these thirty-ish semi-professional dresses
My students appreciate, but I ordered them on sale,
online
And the buttons fall off or they don't fit quite right.
The temperature dropping below 70 degrees leads me to
these
Long socks and leggings, thick bulky sweaters,
And I want to buy a house for the dog I don't have yet,
Raise money for charity.

For my teacher ID, the photographer asked me to take
my mask off
And it felt like peeling off my face.
I even take selfies with it, pretend its intentional
fashion,
A joke or something. I mean, as a woman,
I appreciate only applying makeup on the top portion of
my face,
And, despite this, I can survive this. I have survived.
I am no longer struggling.

Kaitlyn Bolyard

A Woman Who Knows the Way
September 25

The pregnant woman finally in labor, a spectacle,
Still wearing hollowed-out hoop earrings as they rush
her in.
"I'd like to listen," she says, oddly calm, "to my favorite
music,"
Which turns out to be an obscure Russian percussion,
Beat out on giant drums larger than her swollen
stomach.

The intended midwife, feeling useless, squirrels healing
crystals
From her voluminous skirts, placing them strategically
around the room,
Each a faint, pastel hue. She mutters, remembering,
another birth,
When the sunlight caught each stone, casting a rainbow
over the womb.
She never explains her brand of astrology, only lives by
it.

The agnostic mother-to-be figures it can't hurt to use
"natural" methods
Appreciates the colorful, middle-aged woman working
swiftly
As the pain begins to move.
She reaches for the wrinkled hand when the real labor
starts,
Grateful for a guide down this unknown path,
Another woman who already knows the way.

Our Separate Bodies

September 27

Been feeling tired and ugly lately, my clothes don't fit
Because I'm not fit and I'm sick of it
Want to run away from this, but don't want to run,
Sweat dripping from my pores like I'm mostly liquid
I mean I'm mostly liquid
I mean what holds me together anyway?

I wonder how many 36-year-olds wear lingerie everyday
Or lacy bras and thongs – I keep seeing ads that make
me think
Uh, ma'am…does that even cover anything?
I'm still waiting for my spiritual awakening
For something that makes sense, feels real and true.

Truth be told, if I heard the lyrics in a song
I might believe it. If I tasted all the flavors of White Claw
They'd still be identical to me. They're always identical:
Every bottle blonde Barbie with the fake tan and fake
boobs
And fake smile and fake everything.
Every moment the same, a fight or flight crisis flashing
by.

No one tells you marriage is hard,
That you work at it every day.
They assume its happily ever after and then you never
have to
Think about it. Just keep dreaming instead of going on
living.
Following the example of your parents, if you had them,
Of those who were willing to stick it out through

Kaitlyn Bolyard

Every what-the-hell-should-we-eat-for-dinner
disagreement.
And we don't even have kids to deal with – although
maybe
That's why couples do have kids, just to have a
distraction from the daily
How-was-your-day, to have something else to talk about
for a change.

And I wonder how we'll change, how we'll age together,
Far from gracefully, how wrinkles will crease my face,
How my body will eventually betray me.
I already see it starting, I already feel my flesh falling
away from my bones
Until my thin, white skeleton shows.

I have these dreams, dancing naked and feeling suddenly
ashamed
That I don't look the way he remembers me
That first fateful night. But it was dark, and we weren't
really looking,
Were we? Just feeling. Letting ourselves fall into each
other.
Letting go of our separate bodies.

Big Ole Mood
September 29

This latest job had no perquisites, apparently,
They just trusted my good vibes and prayers,
The spell I cast over them, my mastery.
At 31, I tried to be a king,
An entire hive mind of bees,
I'm sorry no one was prepared for me.
I haven't really been present since then,
Except in therapy.

I've only ever been desired sexually,
Never romantically. Thought maybe
I could buy some sex appeal from Walgreens,
Change my scene. I really do hate it here,
In my cabin in the woods, with Jelani.
She could turn a good night into a great one,
But never for me.

You and me -
We can watch each other grow.
Push out of this paper bag, this darkness
Keeping us trapped, unfulfilled, unhappy.
I don't like to agree, makes disagreements too easy.
Instead, I'm thinking about becoming a life coach,
Maybe in France, where no one will understand me.

No one really walks into a walk-in cooler,
Just runs in and screams. It's a primal sort of
Self-care. A big-ole mood echoing back at you.

Kaitlyn Bolyard

Acknowledgements

This book would not have been possible without the encouragement and very real help from my husband, Joel Bolyard. When others (including him) were telling me I needed to collect all these poems into one place, I complained that it would be too much work to find them all. Instead of brushing it off, he took this as a challenge, and for Christmas compiled all of them (pulling from my social media and three abandoned blogs) into one document. It should be noted that my mother-in-law, Sue Bolyard, also helped with this process. I am eternally grateful for their help and dedication, and I think this book simply wouldn't have happened without them.

Kaitlyn Bolyard

About the Author

Kaitlyn Bolyard's poetry has been published in *Moss Piglet, Straylight, Offerings, Children Churches & Daddies,* and *Blackwidow's Web of Poetry.* She also has a second book of poetry, *Inklings,* which was published in 2004. She teaches in the Writing, Rhetoric & Discourse department at DePaul University in Chicago, IL, and lives in Southeastern WI with her husband.

www.ingramcontent.com/pod-product-compliance
Lightning Source LLC
Chambersburg PA
CBHW060523130626
46553CB00002B/623